SMARTER CHARTS

K-2

SMARTER CHARTS

K-2

Optimizing an Instructional Staple to Create
INDEPENDENT READERS and WRITERS

Marjorie Martinelli ✳ *Kristine Mraz*

HEINEMANN
Portsmouth, NH

Heinemann
361 Hanover Street
Portsmouth, NH 03801–3912
www.heinemann.com

Offices and agents throughout the world

The authors and publisher wish to thank those who have generously given permission to reprint borrowed material:

Book cover from *Harry the Dirty Dog* by Gene Zion, illustrated by Margaret Bloy Graham. Text copyright © 1956 by Eugene Zion, renewed 1984. Illustration copyright © 1956 by Margaret Bloy Graham, renewed 1984. Published by HarperCollins Publishers, New York. Used by permission of the publisher.

Library of Congress Cataloging-in-Publication Data
Martinelli, Marjorie.
  Smarter charts, K–2 : optimizing an instructional staple to create
independent readers and writers / Marjorie Martinelli and Kristine Mraz.
      p. cm.
  Includes bibliographical references.
  ISBN–13: 978-0-325-04342-5
  ISBN–10: 0-325-04342-6
 1. Language arts (Primary) —Audio-visual aids. 2. Visual education.
I. Mraz, Kristine. II. Title.
  LB1528.M297 2012
  372.6—dc23   2012022779

Editor: Zoë Ryder White
Production: Patty Adams
Cover and interior design: Monica Ann Crigler
Cover and interior photographer: Jesse Angelo
Author photograph: Tom Martinelli
Typesetter: Monica Ann Crigler
Manufacturing: Steve Bernier

Printed in the United States of America on acid-free paper

16 15 14   VP   4 5

Dedications

For my husband, Tom,
who keeps me nourished
both body and soul.

♡ Marjorie Martinelli

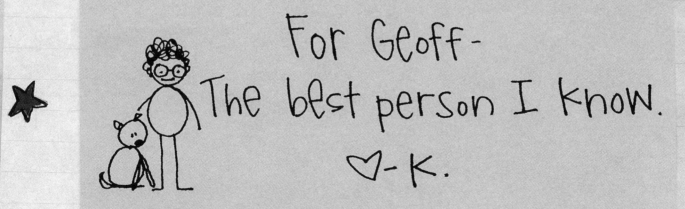

For Geoff-
The best person I know.

♡ -K.

CONTENTS

Acknowledgments

No book is written in isolation, and we are grateful to and want to thank many people. We are indebted to Lucy Calkins, who first suggested we write a book on charts, for reading our proposal, and for cheering us on. We thank Kate Montgomery at Heinemann, who not only encouraged us to submit a proposal but set us up with Margaret LaRaia, who actually got this book off the ground due to her enthusiasm for the project, her probing questions, and her optimistic perseverance. Thanks to Melanie Brown for suggesting the two of us team up in the first place and to Maggie Beattie and Jane Bean-Folkes for being our first readers. Their initial tips and excitement for the project made us feel like this book was actually possible.

Our love and thanks go to our editor, Zoe White, whose gentle tone, keen eye, and quick smile made writing this book pure pleasure. The weekends spent poring over draft after draft while sipping tea and coffee at Café Almondine in Park Slope created a bond that will not soon be broken. She helped us complete our dream and polished it to a shine we never imagined possible.

We feel so fortunate to be among such supportive colleagues at the Teachers College Reading and Writing Project, who lift us up intellectually and nurture us with friendship. There are too many to mention here, but know we are thinking of each and every one of you.

This book came to life visually thanks to the generous spirit of Cheryl Tyler, principal of PS 277 in the Bronx and all her amazing staff. We are particularly indebted to the seven teachers who opened up their classrooms to us and whose children's delightful faces light up the pages of this book. Thank you, Ali Siotkas, Carly Wotman, Robyn Levy, Cara Biggane, Alyssa Newman, Lauren Petrovich, and Joseph Weaver. A big, big thanks to Emily Jones, TCRWP intern extraordinaire, whose patience and persistence made sure no stone was left unturned. And tremendous gratitude goes to Jesse Angelo, our photographer, for treating our charts like fine art and for finding the beauty in everyday classroom moments.

The book production team at Heinemann, headed up by Patty Adams, understood from the beginning our hopes and dreams for this book and used all their creative spirit and talent to make the book both beautiful and user-friendly. Monica Ann Crigler, book designer extraordinaire, quilted all our bits and pieces into a beautiful thing to behold, while Patty and Cindy Ann Black polished it until it shone.

Kristine can't find enough words to thank her husband, Geoff, who single-handedly kept her sane, happy, and hopeful when times got a little rocky. He is possibly the only reason she still has all of her hair and most of it is still brown. As far as best friends/husbands go, Kristine couldn't imagine a more patient, kind, or creative one. Kristine would also like to thank her mom for being her first (and best) teacher.

Marjorie is just as thankful for her husband, Tom, who made sure she ate, left the house for walks in the fresh air (if only to the grocery store), and kept her laughing. Marjorie also thanks her daughters, Christina and Katherine, and son-in-law, Evan, for their never-ending encouragement and positive energy. And her mother, who has always believed in following one's dreams.

As we have traveled from school to school charting our way across the United States, Europe, and Asia, we continue to be inspired and appreciative of teachers and their creativity with charts the world over. Thanks to all the teachers who have followed us so faithfully on our website, Chartchums (chartchums.wordpress.com) and cheered us on. Teachers are our heroes for all they do to make sure their students not only learn, but love learning. This book is for you.

Introduction

"**Y**ou should write a book on charts," we have heard many teachers say while pulling out cell phones to photograph the sample charts used to supplement a workshop on reading or writing. The star of the show has repeatedly been the charts themselves—charts that were created to help children understand the many concepts and strategies being taught during a reading or writing workshop. The surprising thing about this is that charts are something most teachers make. Most teachers know about charts. Most teachers have made hundreds of charts. Most teachers hang charts from every available space in the classroom. Why then did all these teachers want our charts? What was new or different about our charts? Weren't we like every other teacher who simply had made hundreds of charts during her professional career and felt that charts were a necessary part of teaching?

But then we started to think, "What *if* we wrote a book about charts?" We had presented several workshops on creating charts. We had worked with teachers across the country on developing clear and effective charts. But still, one question kept nagging us: What did we have to say about charts that might be new or useful or interesting? It didn't help our confidence when we went online and found there were more than ten million Internet sites on charts. Millions of teachers making charts. Millions of companies selling charts. Millions of charts out there in the world. As we traveled from classroom to classroom and website to website, we saw that many of the charts found had to do with rules, regulations, and organization. Charts often "tell" children what to do, rather than "show" children how and why to do something. Whether teacher-created or commercially prepared, charts are everywhere and a way of life in the classroom. So began our search to find out why.

Kristine still remembers that first visit to the teachers' store, days before teaching her first classroom of second graders. She pored over the chart displays: There were seating charts, attendance charts, behavior charts, incentive charts, reward charts, chore charts, fact charts, flowcharts, KWL (What do I **know**? What do I **want** to know? What did I **learn**?) charts, anchor charts, vocabulary charts, pie charts, Lexile charts, behavior modification charts, and on and on. "What will I need? What will my kids need?" she thought. As she walked out with a cart full of charts, she began to wonder, "Have I put the chart before the horse?" At the end of that first year as Kristine packed up one dusty, unused chart after another, she realized that the chart can't come before the child.

Once Kristine moved away from her unused, pricey store-bought charts, she started making charts to support the actual instruction happening in the classroom. Being a perfectionist, she would make the charts at home and put them up as needed, sometimes making a chart for the whole month of instruction and hanging it on the first day of a unit. This practice stopped in its tracks with the realization that the students were no more likely to look at those handmade charts than the commercially created ones purchased at the teacher store. They might have been cheaper, but they took a lot of time to make. This realization led her to phase 3 in her chart-making evolution: actually involving the students in the creation of the charts, as well as teaching children to interact with the charts within the classroom environment.

Involving children in the developing and evolving classroom environment is not a new idea. When Loris Malaguzzi first began to develop the Italian preschools now known globally as Reggio Emilia, he placed a major emphasis on the classroom environment. He called the environment "the third educator," along with the teachers and the parents, and believed that "in order to act as an educator for the child, the environment has to be flexible: it must undergo frequent modification by the children and the teachers in order to remain up-to-date and responsive to their needs to be protagonists in constructing their knowledge" (Gandini 1998, 177). We have visited many classrooms over many years where teachers have created such responsive environments by making charts that are current and clear. We have learned much from these teachers about the use and purpose of classroom charts, which you will see evidence of across these pages. Consider this book a consciousness-raising effort aimed to elevate charts to a level of necessity— not just because we teachers are told to, but because we have found them to be incredibly helpful tools, full of information, and truly the third teacher in the room.

Once, when Marjorie was a second-grade teacher, a new student, Sandy, arrived in her room late into the fall. She sat him with Alyssa, another student in her classroom, during writing workshop, knowing Alyssa would look after him. As Marjorie scrambled to find another chair, another folder, another math book, she noticed out of the corner of her eye Alyssa leading Sandy by the hand, giving him a tour of each and every writing chart in the room. As they neared the "Starting a New Book?" chart, Marjorie edged a little closer to catch Alyssa saying, "When you get your paper you have to [insert the tune of '(Shake, Shake, Shake) Shake Your Booty' by KC and the Sunshine Band here] Think, think, think! Sketch, sketch, sketch! Write your story!" Sandy looked a little mystified at

the impromptu performance and said, "Write a story about what?" Alyssa smiled knowingly, and said, "Oh, the chart for *that* is over here!" As she pointed toward the "Need an Idea?" chart, Marjorie began to understand that both Alyssa and the chart had become "third teachers" in the room.

Our Beliefs About Teaching and Learning

Though this book has principles and techniques that cross over subject areas, its heart lies with the big ideas of reading and writing workshop as developed by Donald Murray, Donald Graves, and Lucy Calkins. Woven throughout the work of these giants of education is an emphasis on independence, choice, and a celebration of the process of reading and writing. Children read and write daily and are taught the work of reading and writing. As Lucy Calkins says in the *Art of Teaching Writing* (1994), our job is to "teach the writer, not the writing." You don't need to be teaching with reading and writing workshop to use the ideas in this book for making great charts. It is our hope that no matter what teaching framework you, the chart maker, use, you'll learn the skills and strategies necessary to create tools that maximize student independence, encourage choice, and celebrate the problem-solving process along the way.

Think about the charts in this book as mentor texts. We learned from Frank Smith in his groundbreaking book, *Joining the Literacy Club* (1983), to "read like a writer in order to learn how to write like a writer." Similarly, read the charts that follow as a writer of charts by paying attention to structure, details, word choice, style, and sentence structure. And remember, the chart you look at might be on ways to generate writing topics, but instead of focusing on the content of the chart, think about the process, the craft, the purpose, and then think how you could transfer these same ideas to any chart, in any subject. Craft can be imitated and learned, whether you are left-brained or right-brained. Most importantly, we hope you become as enchanted with charts as we have become.

Charting Our Course: The Questions That Guide Our Process

Whether you love them or find them a burden, charts are an expected norm in most classrooms today. Charts are often an indication of the quality of instruction happening in each classroom and have even become a standard part of the evaluative process. Administrative checklists often include charts among the categories listed and many administrators want to see them everywhere, for every subject. Ideally, these charts support children and are responsive to their needs. But what kinds of charts? How many charts? Where to display charts? How much print should be on charts? How long should charts remain on display? Can the same charts be used year after year? Such questions lead to two possible scenarios: an absence of charts, or, like in many classrooms, such a proliferation of charts that the only way to continue hanging them involves standing on a desk and using a yardstick to perch the chart on the highest reaches of the wall, a problem sometimes called "print pollution," or too much of a good thing. What is a teacher to do?

These questions led us to do some research, which quickly pointed us toward multiple paths: brain research, design theory, and principles of learning. But these multiple paths also kept intersecting and overlapping. Cognitive and educational psychologist Jerome Bruner stated forty years ago that "we easily become overwhelmed by complexity and clutter" (Bruner 1971, 4). Almost twenty years later, Edward R. Tufte, a key figure in the world of analytical and visual design, declared that "clutter and confusion are failures of design, not attributes of information" (Tufte 1990, 51). And just the other day, we watched a first grader report back to her teacher that she could not locate the word *said* on the word wall because, with arms splayed widely apart, "there's like a million S words up there!" Both the work in classrooms and the research in these fields have brought us to a few big ideas.

Advertisers Know What They Are Doing

The other day, Kristine walked with her niece past a Subway restaurant. Almost simultaneously they broke into "Five . . . five . . . five-dollar foot-looooooong!" Looking over at her niece, Kristine was almost jealous, thinking, "Why can't I get that kind of recall in the classroom?!" As she told this story, we started talking about what the advertising world knows about making things stick that we could learn from and use in the classroom. We thought that there must be reasons some charts seem to be more effective than others, just like some advertisements catch your attention and stick with you whether you want them to or not.

To find some possible answers, we turned to the areas that make it their business to understand what makes something memorable: the world of art, advertising, and commercial design.

The commercial world has mastered the art of communicating large amounts of information and ideas with a few words and a few images. Perception, usability, and appeal are key components considered by advertisers and designers alike to get their messages across and to make a lasting impact on their targeted audiences. There is a wonderful reference book on design, *Universal Principles of Design* (2010) by William Lidwell, Jill Butler, and Kritina Holden, which presents 125 design principles that explain why humans respond the way they do to the visual, audible forms of communication that compel us to attend to some products more than others and makes this design knowledge available to all. Many design qualities we all know intuitively, for example, "A picture is worth a thousand words." But how much more powerful to learn that researchers refer to the power of pictures as the "picture superiority effect" and have found that recall is enhanced beyond that of words alone, especially when exposure time is limited and the pictures are clearly recognizable.

For example, one resourceful teacher, Kathy Soto, found it far quicker to transition her children to their reading spots by simply flashing a picture of a book, rather than repeating the same oral directions day after day. Or that highlighting and bolding are effective attention-getting devices if used sparingly, no more than 10 percent of the visible design (Lidwell et al. 2010). Just think back to your college days when many of you probably highlighted entire paragraphs or pages only to find when studying for an exam you were forced to reread entire sections because you didn't know what was actually important in that highlighted paragraph. And how about "exposure effect," which has shown that repeated exposure leads to familiarity and acceptance (Lidwell et al. 2010). It is hard to imagine, for example, that the Eiffel Tower or the Guggenheim Museum has ever been reviled, but it took years of exposure before they became accepted and revered as cultural landmarks by the general public. Or even to remember now how foreign the multiplication table looked when we first laid eyes on this now familiar tool.

Edward Tufte takes great pleasure in pointing out how words, numbers, and images have aided in understanding complex ideas for thousands of years. In his visually stunning book *Beautiful*

Evidence (2006), he states that "evidence that bears on questions of any complexity typically involves multiple forms of discourse" (83). He proceeds to show by example how such intellectual luminaries as Galileo, Dürer, and da Vinci used high percentages of images along with words, numbers, and diagrams to explain the stars, measurement, and anatomy in ways that are compelling and memorable. What an exquisite thought that we could lift up the lowly school chart and lay it alongside the works of such great teachers in our efforts to help our students understand important information simply by using a high percentage of images, words, numbers, and diagrams.

A few other principles of design long considered important when it comes to ads or charts include readability, legibility, constancy, clarity, balance, consistency, icons, patterns, comparison, color, and accessibility. Classroom charts that use these same principles as the commercial world also receive the same benefits. Alternatively, we mustn't forget that the world of advertising also uses these tools to convert and colonize, rather than inspire deeper understandings and independence. We chose to subvert these tools for the greater purpose of educating and empowering students.

It's All in Your Head: Charts May Not Be Rocket Science, But They Are Brain Science

But why do things like pictures and limited bolding make a difference? Why does Kristine's niece remember the five-dollar foot-long song, yet fail to remember the value of a quarter? Why, also, can Kristine never remember the zip code of her mom's house, yet at a moment's notice sing "Two whole beef patties, special sauce, lettuce, cheese, pickles, onion on a sesame bun" all with complicated hand gestures? It all comes down to the brain.

Research into how the brain functions has led to increased understandings and many explanations for the various ways children respond to the instruction teachers present and offers answers to the many questions teachers have concerning the diversity of children who cross our paths each year. Knowing what stimulates the brain to attend and remember information is critical to understanding why some charts help and others are ignored. Such familiar things as prior knowledge and engagement can make the difference between what information is used and what is forgotten.

One thing that aids memory first and foremost is perception. Perception is often thought of as what we see with our eyes, but it actually includes all the senses: sight, sound, smell, taste, and touch. You sense you are near the ocean when you hear seagulls squawking, smell a salty seaweed odor, and feel sandy grit under your feet, long before you actually set eyes upon the aqua shoreline. But prior knowledge also comes into play; if you had never been to the ocean before, never experienced the sound of seagulls, never smelled seaweed, never felt sand under your feet, you might not have made such an accurate perception. New information combined with stored information contributes to our understanding of each situation we experience. Using familiar representations on charts, like an eye or a mouth, can help in creating meaning for the new information we are trying to help children remember. And as Howard Gardner reminds us, "It is essential to portray the topic in a number of ways to call in a range of intelligences, skills and interests" (1999, 176).

Another important aspect of memory is attention. A familiar lament often heard from teachers is, "Samantha never pays attention to anything I say." Patricia Wolfe in her helpful book on translating brain research into classroom practice, *Brain Matters* (2001), suggests that novelty, intensity, and movement are effective stimuli that can increase attention, which helps explain why children who are engaged and motivated remember more. The teacher who dons Groucho Marx glasses just prior to a lesson on punctuation rules definitely gets her students' attention. Raising the volume of Mozart's Fifth Symphony at the end of writing workshop will definitely get students' attention. Flashing the overhead lights on and off also works to get attention. You are probably nodding your head in acknowledgment and thinking, "Yep, those things work for me." Unfortunately, Wolfe adds a major caveat: Novelty, intensity, and movement are only effective for a short time. Once any one of these conditions is used often enough to become habit, the effectiveness becomes mute, unless it also contains some emotionally relevant response or vivid memory imprinted on our brains. For example, role-plays, simulations, guest speakers, and field trips bring experiences to life and aid in memory by combining experience, emotion, and actions. You can incorporate these memorable elements into the charts you make and use them in your classrooms to keep the charts refreshed and memorable.

Visual Literacy: A Picture Really *Is* Worth a Thousand Words But Is Faster to Read

Much has been written in current professional literature about what is termed "visual literacy." Visual literacy is the ability to access information that is presented in such forms as pictures, diagrams, maps, charts, symbols, and signs. It is in the world around us, in the print media, and in the electronic media. No matter where in the world you travel, for example, not only can you find a restroom, but you can distinguish the men's room from the women's room by the graphic representations that symbolize a man and a woman. In print media and electronic media, we are deluged with information presented in the form of graphs, diagrams, signs, maps, images, and icons. They can be still and stable, like the red and white Target logo, as well as rapidly moving and changing, like the Target television commercials. In addition, with constant repetition they have become a source of automatic recall for many complex concepts. This is the only world our students have known.

There is a reason for the proliferation of visuals in a highly literate world. Visuals increase any student's capacity to remember information. Although smell may be the strongest memory, no one has yet invented the scratch and sniff chart (although this may be closer than we think). Visual memory is the second strongest, and one that we can use. When information is presented only in spoken form, 10 percent is recalled after seventy-two hours. Add visuals and 65 percent is recalled in that same time period (Medina 2008). It is a form of presenting information in the classroom that teachers need to grab hold of and use in order to stay current and effective. As you consider what to put on a chart, know the importance of visuals to capture people's attention. Icons and symbols are particularly effective because they can become universal in our schools, just like the bathroom symbols are universal in airports across the world.

Above All, Charts Engage and Lead Students Toward Independence

Using all of the elements we've described thus far results in beautiful, eye-catching, accessible charts, but it doesn't provide the whole answer to what makes charts a necessary tool in every classroom. When so many professionals make use of a tool, you have to think there must be some very good reasons for its use. Why do teachers use charts with such abandon in every classroom? Why have they become second nature and an expected artifact of our teaching? It might be because, above all, charts teach children to be independent problem solvers, and is there anything more important than that? As Peter Johnston explains in *Choice Words* (2004) when he talks of children having agency and a can-do attitude, "Children should leave school with a sense that if they act, and act strategically, they can accomplish their goals" (29). Charts are meant to aid in solving typical problems that often arise. In other words, the chart is for those who can do—using a chart is a can-do action!

Of course, this is easier said than done. Helping children understand we are here to help, not hinder, their learning is an idea that needs to be made public and cried out loud and clear to the students in front of us. Although this may seem obvious, just ask Cynthia Hernandez, a second-grade teacher in New York City. She was conferring with Maria, who was writing a book on shoes, and wanted to prompt her to use the chart on ways to elaborate an information book. When she suggested Maria look to the chart for some ways to teach more about her subject, Maria took one quick look at the chart and then turned back to Cynthia with a surprised look on her face. "It's like you're giving us all the answers!" she exclaimed. In actuality, Cynthia was working more like the search engine Google in this instance, providing links for Maria to follow so she could help herself.

As you move away from store-bought charts and begin making charts that support the instruction in your classroom, or as you seek to make your own classroom charts more powerful, you might find yourself frustrated in a variety of ways. When will you make the charts? Where will they hang? What will go on them? What if nobody uses them? Breathe deep and know we have been there. We have also learned that you don't need to be perfect, just thoughtful.

Marjorie began by trying to make charts perfectly as she taught—"perfectly" being the issue that made this system break down. She simply could not write and illustrate fast enough to keep pace. Children would ask things like, "What does that say?" and when looking at her quick drawing of a book, "Why did you put a house on the chart?" It was frustrating, but ultimately, challenge can be the best teacher! She found a few solutions that worked, but more importantly through this process she discovered what mattered more was that children were engaged in the process of making the chart, making it more memorable from its birth. She started to see children go back to the charts and talk about them to each other. "It's on the chart," one child would say to another, as Marjorie would nearly fall over in shock.

No matter what, children need to be active participants in the making of the chart. The coauthorship invests children and allows for the chart to be seen as belonging to them, just as much as you. A chart does not just appear; it is born through the hard work of both teacher and students, and that gives it life in the classroom. The charts we share with you in this book and the techniques and stories we provide came from this classroom life and from the classrooms we have worked in over the years.

A Field Guide to the Charts in This Book

There are a variety of charts contained within the covers of this book. The different types of charts serve different purposes in classrooms. You do not need to have one of each type, and you may find that you make one type much more frequently and another hardly at all. The "Types of Charts" table will aid you in identifying types, in understanding a bit about the purpose, and in creating your own charts (also see Appendix A). We have labeled the types of charts as they appear in the book.

As we lead you through an examination of the qualities of good charting, you'll see the different types of charts represented in the table. We chose to organize our charts (and our book) based on the qualities of good charting because we aim to teach the *thinking* that leads to successful chart making regardless of artistic or any other creative talents. We wanted to isolate elements of successful charts and present them in a way that would help readers replicate the qualities of successful charts, rather than the content. The charts in this book are designed to be accessible to various grade levels and developmental needs. As you read forward, take a deep breath and plunge in. Far more important than perfection is the thinking that goes into the charts, and ultimately, the independence and agency strong charts will encourage in your students.

A Field Guide to Literacy Charts

Type of Chart	Purpose	Notes	Example (see front cover flap)
Routine	Teaches a routine or behavior to students	• Often numbered • Written like a how-to • Includes photographs of students in action • Most often made at the beginning of the year	**Fig. A.** "How to Set Up for Writers' Workshop" chart
Strategy	Records a list of strategies for a big skill	• Not numbered • Students self-select the strategy that matches what they need to do • Grows over multiple lessons	**Fig. B.** A strategy chart
Process	Breaks a big skill into a sequence of steps	• Can be numbered or sometimes represented in a circle • Students need to do each of the steps to complete the process • Usually taught in one lesson	**Fig. C.** "Writers Plan Our Stories" chart
Exemplar	Shows specific strategies or skills in context	• Usually a shared or interactive writing piece • Teacher annotates where a certain skill is with a big sticky note or note in the margin	**Fig. D.** Joshua's piece of writing has been annotated by the teacher in order to use it as an exemplar.
Genre	Teaches students the elements of a specific genre	• Usually built collaboratively with students after studying some sample of the genre • Grows over multiple lessons	**Fig. E.** "Fiction Stories Have" chart

Charts can be categorized in several ways.

Directions for the Reader

In the Table of Contents you can see that the book is organized into three main sections, each focused on one important aspect of smarter chart creation and use. Each section begins with a large, overarching question, then lists several specific questions teachers frequently ask about charts, and then presents various techniques that will clarify these common queries. Within each main section, you'll find a "Charts in Action" feature. These features provide a window into real, live charting classrooms. We'll share transcripts of interactions between teachers and children as teachers help children use charts in a variety of ways, using a variety of teaching methods, both in whole-class situations and with small, targeted groups. We'll pull out specific charting tips alongside these transcripts. Photographs of actual charts help illustrate each section.

The focus of Section 1: "What Do I Put on My Charts?" is on the language, vocabulary, and visuals that make charts accessible and memorable to children based on age and developmental stages. Here you will find suggestions for coming up with clear and catchy headings, considerations for determining the amount of print to use on a chart, choosing vocabulary that has the biggest impact, and the types of visuals that will support these messages.

In Section 2: "How Can I Help My Students Use the Charts Independently?" we acknowledge the realities of limited time and limited space and will help you find some possible solutions to these age-old dilemmas most teachers face. In addition, we share some fun ways to make charts memorable by using music, chants, and rhymes. And we also show how we can use charts to help children make connections between reading and writing.

And last, but not least, Section 1: "How Do I Assess the Success of My Charts?" dives into the deep waters of assessment by considering self-assessment. This includes tips for helping children self-assess themselves and their work using the charts in the classroom. We also show how teachers can self-assess using those same charts by considering effectiveness and relevancy, then making decisions about which charts to revise and which charts to retire. This brings us back to the concepts brought up in Section 1 concerning clarity, in Section 2 regarding realities, and now in Section 3 assessing effectiveness.

We have included tips and hints that have helped us along the way, and we hope they will help you along the way as well. Each section includes two "Charts in Action" samples that show how a chart is developed or used with students to reinforce and support the concepts being taught. It also provides tips for how to make the chart memorable and helpful so it will be used in the future as well.

Although each quality of good charting is isolated in a section and given its time to shine, you will find the qualities also referred to across each section. Like any good advertisement, a chart uses all of these qualities simultaneously. You do not need to read this book in any particular order; rather, you can skip around to all the sections to create your own pathway through the chart-making adventure based on your questions and needs. Most importantly, experiment! Just like cooks start with a recipe, following each step exactly, until eventually they make the dish their own, to match their own tastes, and the tastes of those they are cooking for, we encourage you to do the same with these charts and all the others you create, keeping the principles of strong, effective charts forefront in your mind. Happy charting!

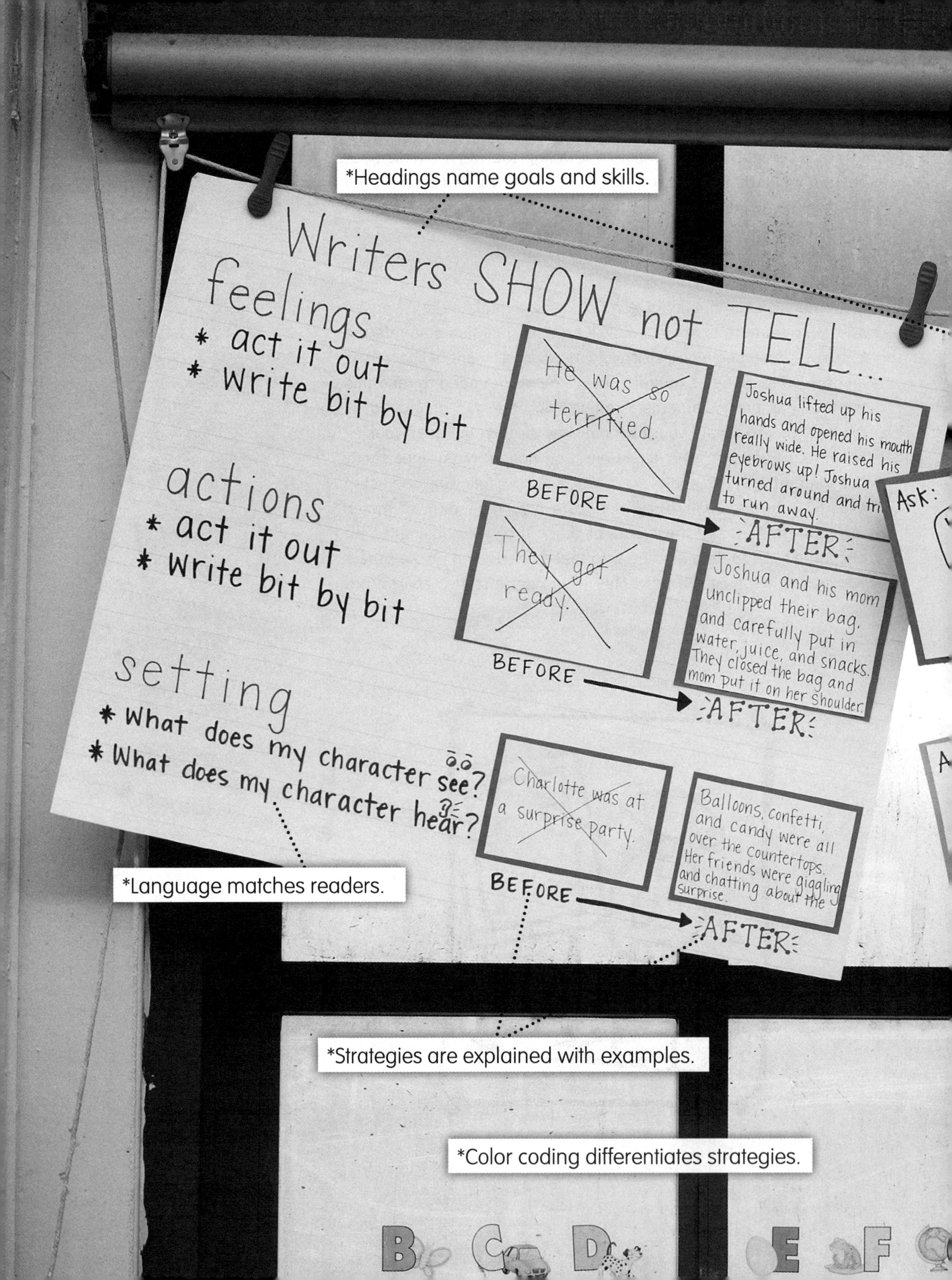

*Headings name goals and skills.

Writers SHOW not TELL...

feelings
* act it out
* write bit by bit

actions
* act it out
* write bit by bit

setting
* What does my character see?
* What does my character hear?

BEFORE
He was so terrified.

AFTER
Joshua lifted up his hands and opened his mouth really wide. He raised his eyebrows up! Joshua turned around and tri to run away.

BEFORE
They got ready.

AFTER
Joshua and his mom unclipped their bag, and carefully put in water, juice, and snacks. They closed the bag and mom put it on her shoulder.

BEFORE
Charlotte was at a surprise party.

AFTER
Balloons, confetti, and candy were all over the countertops. Her friends were giggling and chatting about the surprise.

Ask:

*Language matches readers.

*Strategies are explained with examples.

*Color coding differentiates strategies.

B C D E F

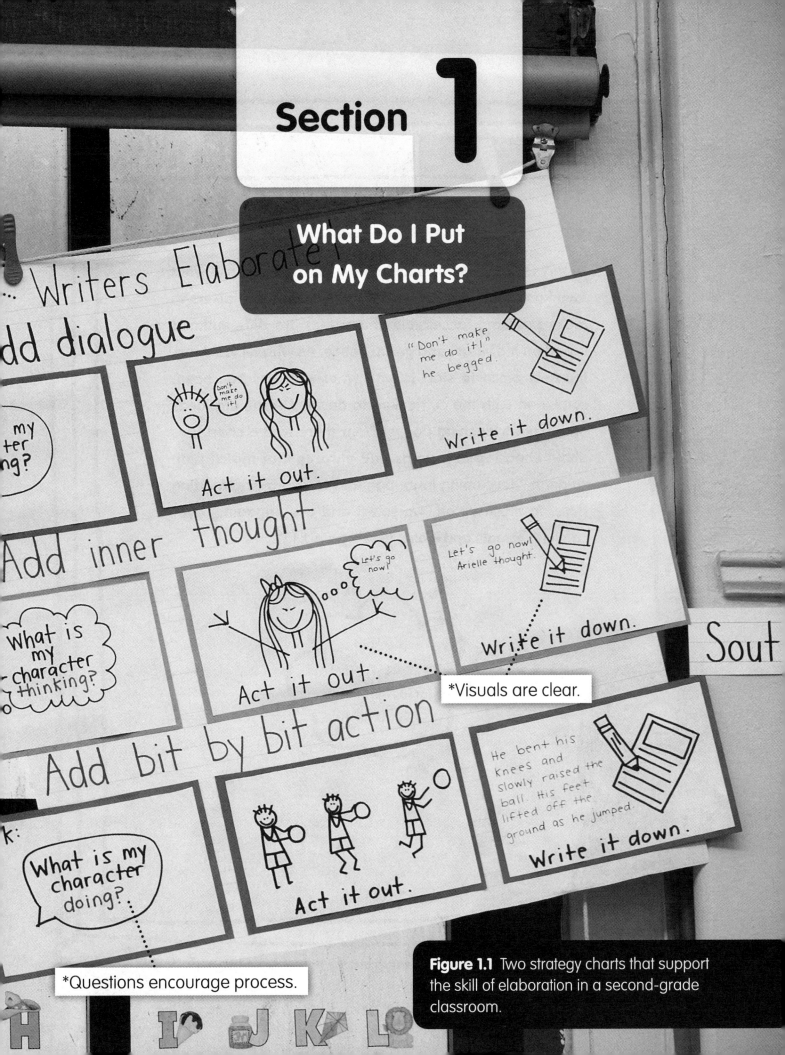

Section 1

What Do I Put on My Charts?

Figure 1.1 Two strategy charts that support the skill of elaboration in a second-grade classroom.

In this section, we will explore how teachers can use what they know about their students as readers and talkers to make powerful, accessible charts that are differentiated based on individual and group needs. As with all teaching, the best place to start is with what your children need, combined with the curriculum to develop some big ideas and explicit teaching points. From there to the chart, it is about choosing key words and phrases that match both students' developing language and their growing reading skills. To top it all off, we select and use engaging, eye-catching visuals and icons. (See Figure 1.1.)

With all things, there is never perfection, only possibility.

Write Headings That Address Common Problems

The supermarket in Marjorie's neighborhood recently underwent some renovation, and while they were remodeling, the signs above the aisles were removed. Because this had been her supermarket for years, she went forth, list in hand, untroubled by the upheaval. Twenty minutes later, her cart was still empty, her hair in disarray, and she was no longer so confident in her memory recall. Where was the rice? The cereal? The spices? Without the aisle signs she was lost, wandering, and unable to locate anything she wanted. In frustration, Marjorie left and went out to dinner with her husband instead.

Thoughtful organization and clear labeling are essential components of creating independence. The world around us bears evidence to this fact. Airports, stores, restaurants are all designed to help people find what they need with minimum assistance. A classroom's charts can lean on this work in the retail world. A chart's heading, much like a sign above a grocery aisle, signals what information a child will find there. What the heading says depends on a few factors.

What Are You Teaching?

Depending on purpose and unit, you will have different kinds of charts in your classroom. Just as a grocery store with no aisle signs is confusing and unmanageable, all of one's teaching on a chart can be just as hard for children to navigate. When Kristine first began teaching, she had one chart titled "Writers Have Lots of Tools to Help Us Write All Our Stories" that was so long it filled two pieces of chart paper taped together. It did little more than block good real estate in the classroom. When asked a question that she thought might be on the chart, it often took several minutes to locate the teaching on the list. To avoid this, Kristine now plans the goals in her unit, any unit, first, and then the charts needed to support these goals. Before starting to teach any unit, she always asks, "What are the very big ideas I am teaching in this unit?" Or perhaps, "What are the essential and guiding questions that will drive this unit?" Once she has an idea of the three or four big goals, next is to start thinking about how each individual chart

might go. The best goals grow from studying your own students and making smart decisions about where to take them next as readers and writers. The table that follows might help you think about some of the types of goals you want to set in your own classroom. These goals, of course, are just samples, not ones that we suggest you use. Rather, it's the process of making goals that may help you make stronger charts.

When we think about Kristine's epic multipage chart in this light, it is obvious that there was no clear system for children to find support around a certain goal. A tip for writing longer might be next to a strategy for using punctuation. A child would be uncertain how to find a tip or a strategy to reach a certain goal. With independence and ease in mind, we can make a chart much more accessible if we make one chart for each big goal. The heading names the big goal.

The heading will aid children in understanding the purpose and meaning of each chart and allow them to independently identify if they will need to use the chart to help them at that moment. When we think in big goals, it also allows us to think of the teaching that will assist children in reaching the goal. The heading reminds both you and the child what the big work is; the information below the heading will be strategies, steps, and tips to achieve that big work. Because you are working on more than one thing in each unit, it therefore makes sense to have more than one chart. You do not put grocery items and clothing items on the same list because you may not get those from the same place. That idea is true of your charts as well. Identifying your goals and using those to create the headings on your charts will help students make smart choices in the charts they turn to and then in turn the strategies they select to use as readers and writers.

Now How Will You Write It?

Think of charting as demonstrating effective note taking for students. The *heading* is what we write on the top of our paper or next to the roman numerals in our outlines. The heading in an outline is usually not more than a few words. We just want to capture a main idea and move on. The same is true of headings on charts. We can write headings a variety of ways, but what matters most is that it identifies *what* the chart is about, so that children can effectively and independently select the chart that will help them achieve their goals as readers and writers. Headings can be simple phrases or sentences and should represent the language

Areas of Teaching and Sample Goals

Area of Teaching	And That Means . . .	Sample Goals Might Sound Like . . .
Genre	This involves teaching the elements of a specific genre to your students—for example, studying the characteristics of information books to aid students in writing their own information books.	**Writing** Students will be able to identify and use the distinguishing features of nonfiction texts in their own information books. **Reading** Students will identify and use the distinguishing features of nonfiction to read and understand grade-level nonfiction texts.
Reading and writing process	There are many different writing processes in the world, but a common one follows these steps: generate, plan, draft, revise, and edit. The reading process is often described as predict, revise, and confirm. This is true on a word level, page level, and book level.	**Writing** Students will revise writing pieces as they go so that the piece better matches the story they want to tell. **Reading** Readers will monitor as they read to make sure what they read makes sense, sounds right, and looks right.
Qualities of good reading and writing	Regardless of genre, there are qualities that make for good writing. A few of them are: focus, elaboration, craft, and voice. In reading, this might mean: fluency, deep comprehension, literal comprehension.	**Writing** Students will use varied elaboration strategies to develop tension in their stories. **Reading** Students will stop and think about the characters so that they gain a deeper understanding of the text.
Behaviors of readers and writers	Stamina, talking with partners, and building volume are all behaviors of writers and readers. This also covers teaching around problem solving.	**Writing** Students will write for thirty-five minutes every day. **Reading** Students will read for thirty-five minutes every day.

This chart shows areas of teaching and sample goals.

and reading level of your students. You can perhaps imagine a classroom with reading charts that have the following headings: "Partners Talk About . . . ," "We Can Read Even Longer," "Predicting," and "Shopping for Books." Without tons of writing on the top of each chart, it is easy to see what the students are working on in that classroom. In such a classroom, if a child and her reading partner are staring at each other blankly, it would be easy for the partners to find the chart that will give some strategies for getting some book talk up and going. A simple word or phrase can communicate big ideas quite effectively. The following list shows some sample headings that capture the big work clearly and succinctly.

"Getting Ideas"

"Revise Your Work"

"Time to Reread"

"Getting Ready for Writing"

"Reading Partners Can . . ."

"Get to Know Your Character"

Some of the most effective headings on charts are phrased as questions. See Figure 1.2. This is a trick advertisers and authors use all the time to capture our attention, "Are you tired of scrubbing the tub?" the ad asks, and what follows is a miracle answer for the

Figure 1.2 These headings reflect the writing goals of this first-grade classroom.

beleaguered tub scrubber. We can mimic that work in our charts. For a chart that is teaching strategies to predict, rather than calling it "Ways to Predict," we could call it, "Wondering What Happens Next?" Students have to think yes or no, and that helps them determine if this chart is what they actually need to use at this time. Questions engage readers and students alike and begin a conversation between text and student. You can even mimic the questions your children ask on the chart, to help them find answers. Are you constantly being asked, "What can I write about?" Then make your ideas chart have that heading! What about, "I don't know what else to write!"? Then name your elaboration chart: "Wondering what else to write?" A few samples taken from classrooms follow:

"Feeling Done?"

"What Can Partners Do?"

"Stuck on a Tricky Word?"

"What's the Movie in Your Mind?"

These headings deal with some predictable problems found in one first-grade classroom.

To make certain your readers and writers know what the headings say and are aware of the valuable teaching that comes on each chart, you might write the heading together during an interactive writing time. You can introduce the chart, saying, "We are going to be learning a lot about using details in our writing this month. I thought it would make sense for us to start a chart that helps us remember the ways we learn to do that when you are working on your own. Let's think about how the heading for a chart about details might sound." Then together write *only* the question or phrase that will serve as the heading for that chart. Then all month, as you teach strategies for adding details, add those onto the chart.

So, first step to good charts? Knowing what your big goals are for the unit of study. Once that has been identified, you know how many charts you will need to support the work of your readers and writers. Then, decide on how the heading will sound and write it with your students so they will remember the purpose of each chart when they go to access them independently. Next up, we will discuss ensuring your charts are readable and understandable to the students in your room.

Use Written Language That Reflects Students' Reading Levels

Once we have a catchy heading, we need to think about what goes on the rest of the chart. Much of our teaching is often driven by oration. We spend minutes explaining and demonstrating complex tasks, and then, somehow, we have to put that same idea on a chart in a way that a five-, six-, or seven-year-old will be able to use long after the teaching is done. These strategies make up the bulk of each chart. Teachers often ask, "How many words should there be? Should there be a one-word label? A sentence?" Then they ask, "How many labels? How many sentences?" Many of the answers lie in our knowledge of the children in our classrooms. Some thought goes into children's concepts about print (Clay 1985), letter-sound knowledge, and reading levels. A good rule of thumb is to take a look at the books your students are reading. You will want to notice:

- the amount of print on a page
- the size of the print
- the size of the spaces
- the number of lines of print.

If this is what our students can read independently, then it serves as a good mentor for how our charts should read. "Who?" "Where?" and "What?" are short and simple while incorporating sight words that our students probably know as kindergartners. The increase in the amount of words and vocabulary on the first-grade chart reflects what the students in each classroom read independently. (See Figures 1.3 and 1.4.) No matter the chart one makes, the most essential question might be, "What can my students read and understand?"

Even if you have some high-flying readers in your room, you probably don't need more than a sentence or two per strategy to get the point across. Remember, the chart is meant to help with active working memory. Too much print can take away too much time from writing or reading grade-level texts. Much can be communicated in a few simple sentences. Again, think of the billboards and advertisements around you: If the print is too overwhelming, one tends to look away. Power comes from quality and clarity, not quantity of print.

As you think about how to represent your teaching in words, there are a few tips to diminish the amount of words you use on your chart. First, remember that new teaching will be added to a chart that names a big idea already. You do not need to rename the big idea, you just need to write the new bits of information that children will need to remember when trying to work on that goal. In a chart named "Adding Details" you can bullet out the ways to add details as you teach them, without renaming them as details. Another tip is to think about the key nouns and verbs you used as you were teaching. A single word can serve as a powerful trigger for your students of the bigger idea, as long as you have taught the idea in a focus lesson. In that way, a lesson about the importance of drawing and writing about the people who are in your story can perhaps be represented with the simple word "Who?" or the phrase "Who is in your story?"

Choose Vocabulary That Mirrors Students' Oral Language

As children navigate their way through school, they are always treading between the worlds of social language and academic language, between the literal and the abstract, trying to make sense of the world around them. The language we use on charts must also tread these waters, using the social language the children speak and transitioning to the academic language they will need in the future as they develop and grow as students. Marie Clay reminded teachers that children's control of English syntax increases gradually over time and can be an early indicator of understanding. She also taught teachers to listen for the length of utterances each child put forth (Clay 1991). These are clues to how many words children can understand at any given moment. This is where word choice becomes critical as we think about the words and phrases we will use on our charts.

One way to find the "just-right" words and phrases for our charts is to listen to the words children use to define and label what they are learning. Marjorie often talks about when her nephew, Peter, first became enamored with trains. As a one-year-old, he talked excitedly about "choo-choos," a name for trains that came from how they sounded. He then started to refer to trains as "choo-choo trains." It wasn't long before he was distinguishing trains by their functions: steam locomotive, coal burning combine, or diesel

Figure 1.3 "Writers Write" chart

Differentiating Language for Kindergartners and First Graders

The charts in Figures 1.3 and 1.4 support children in a quality of writing: elaboration. The goal in both cases revolves around what details writers include in their stories. These charts are for a narrative writing unit. As you look at them, think about the vocabulary chosen and the way it supports the youngest writers.

Differentiating Language for Kindergarten

In the first chart, *writers write* is a simple and easy phrase that five- and six-year-olds can remember. The phrase serves as an easy entry point into a more complex idea. Then the words *who, where,* and *what* follow as strategies for what writers write about. The simple phrases and the use of sight words enable our youngest writers to elaborate independently. Whenever we make charts for young writers, we tend to use the same type of familiar images and simple phrases borrowed from our students' everyday language. You might even find yourself asking your children, "How should this sound on our chart? What should we say?" Eventually we may change the words to character, setting, and events, but for now, simple means more success.

Differentiating Language for First Grade

In the chart in Figure 1.4, the scaffold of a phrase is changed to better name the goal, "Make It a nailbiter!" This engages the writer in a conversation with herself, "Am I making my story a nail-biter?" The chart provides the strategies to the complex skill of building tension. The simple list of the kindergarten chart has expanded to show the writer a more sophisticated process. More words surround each strategy in this first grade chart, as well as options for the varied levels in many first-grade classrooms. Some students may be working to build tension in their picture, others their words, and some in both. The sample student work serves as a visual scaffold, with the strategy highlighted in both the words and pictures. The goal is to move writers away from needing a teacher to ask for help and instead use the chart to support independent use of the strategies taught.

Figure 1.4 "Make It a Nail-Biter" chart

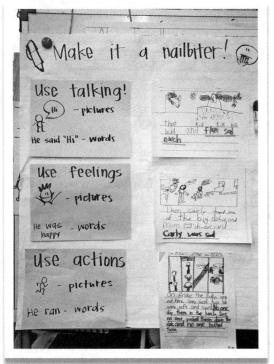

engine. As his train knowledge grew, so did the vocabulary he used to talk about and describe locomotives. Her knowledge also grew with each interaction with this young train enthusiast. The same is true for how charts reflect knowledge of literary language and vocabulary development.

So, remember that word choice can begin with the concrete, the literal, and lead the way to more abstract, inferential words in the future. It begins with listening to the language our children use to define and describe the things they do and use in their world.

Identifying the concrete words that children use every day will not be the only way to help them make the leap toward more abstract and inferential words. To make this type of academic language meaningful, it is imperative that students know what you mean by these words and have experience with the concept. Using a prop, incorporating gestures, using facial expressions and gestures yourself when using academic language can create these experiences for students. These things increase a student's participation, which will also increase the student's understanding and learning (Cappellini 2005). Teaching the language of speaking and writing is essential to having successful writing charts that can be read by your students.

One last example of the importance of teaching what words mean before we use them on charts and in our teaching happened early one September. Kristine was in a first-grade classroom and it was time to bring the workshop to an end. She put her hand up to signal students' attention and then asked them to start wrapping it up. As she scanned the room, she noticed one student, Miguel, heading into the writing center for a fresh booklet. "Miguel?" Kristine asked. "What's up?" He looked over and said, "I need more paper to wrap my story up in." Momentarily stunned, Kristine responded by saying, "Miguel, *wrap it up* is another way to say *time to finish*. You don't need more paper, just put what you have in your folder." His eyes widened. "Ooh," he said, and then looked down at the paper in his hands a little disappointed. "I thought it was gonna be a present."

At times we use language without considering if we have taught and modeled its meaning, and when we assume, well, you have a frustrated first grader trying to wrap a story in a piece of paper when it's time to end writing workshop. Choose your words wisely, teach what they mean, and use them consistently throughout the day . . . and use those same words on your charts.

CHARTS IN ACTION: MAKING THOUGHTFUL LANGUAGE CHOICES ON CHARTS

Charts help keep children active and attuned to what you are teaching (see Figure 1.5). Charts created in front of children add another dimension to your teaching, another modality, by adding visuals and opportunities for repetition of the language. The lesson that follows will show you how a strategy chart is developed with children and how charts can indeed become the third teacher in the room, assisting both you and the children in the learning process.

Lesson Focus: Writers think about places we go all the time, people we know, and things we do to remember stories that have happened in our lives.

Materials:

- A piece of chart paper with the heading already written ("We Dig Up Stories") along with pictures that illustrate the concept "digging up" from *Harry the Dirty Dog*

- "Places I go," "People I know," and "Things I do" written on large sticky notes to hang on the chart

Marjorie begins the focus lesson.

"Writing workshop is a special place where we come together and get to know each other by remembering and sharing our stories and then writing them down so they are never forgotten. We are discovering we have many stories to tell, but

Figure 1.5 The completed strategy chart.

The heading uses kid-friendly language.

Illustrations remind children where the metaphor comes from.

Subheadings use known words to make reading the chart easier.

A variety of strategies provide multiple entry points.

Pictures provide visual examples.

We dig up stories....

HARRY the Dirty Dog

sometimes our stories are buried, like Harry the Dirty Dog's dog brush, so we have to search for them and dig them up again." (See Figure 1.6.)

"Just like Harry digged up his brush!" Ahmed shouts out.

Chart Tips

- Relate your heading to the learning goal. In this case, generating writing ideas independently.

- Make the heading stand out visually.

- Use familiar visuals.

- Prepare some parts ahead of time to save time in the lesson.

- Make the heading catchy and child friendly.

Figure 1.6 This is the strategy chart before the lesson begins.

"Today I am going to teach you one way we can dig up these buried stories is to think about places we go, people we know, and things we do."

Marjorie points to the heading written on the chart paper. Then she adds to the chart by placing prepared signs that say, "Places I go!" "People I know!" and "Things I do!" with pictures that illustrate each concept. The oval shape is a reference to the hole Harry dug to bury his brush. (See Figure 1.7.)

- Place the enlarged sticky notes up when you say the words; this makes the oral instruction visible.

- Construct the chart in front of the students.

- Keep the language clear and friendly to young students.

"Watch how I do this. Hmm . . . where can I find where my stories are buried?"

"Look at the chart!" Marta says helpfully, pointing to the chart.

Marjorie looks again at the chart and touches each sign, pausing, allowing time to think.

Figure 1.7 The strategies are now being added to the chart.

CHARTS IN ACTION

- Model using the chart.

- Give wait time so children are using the chart alongside you.

"Oh, so maybe if I think about places I go all the time I'll dig up some stories. Well . . . I go to school all the time. Let me think about the stories that have happened to me in school. Oh, I remember one time I was trying to help Stefanos turn on the water fountain and I ended up squirting him in the face. Uh-oh! That would be a good story to write about."

"Yeah, that was so funny. Stefanos jumped up so high," Michaela agrees.

Heads nod up and down in agreement.

"Do you see how I thought of a place I go to all the time and then dug deep to remember things that happened to me in that place?"

- Use the same language in your teaching as you use in your chart.

"Hmm . . . Let me see if I can dig some more to remember other stories. Oh, I remember the one time my friend Ms. Davis told me she was moving to another state. I was so sad."

"My friend Joshua moved last summer," Jon adds. "I was really sad, too."

"Yes, Jon, these are the kinds of stories that happen to all of us."

Marjorie points to the heading on the chart and reads the words, then touches the pictures of places, people, and things that represent the stories remembered. She then points to the words and the children join in and say each prompt together.

- Use familiar sight words and language to help children recall the teaching you are doing.

- Repeat. Repeat, and repeat your teaching again using the same language.

- Gesture to the chart as you say the words.

- Engage children to use the language and the chart with you.

"You can do this too whenever you are trying to find more stories to write. Stories are often buried in the places we go, the people we know, and the things we do. All we have to do is dig them up again! You can do this too. Let's try it right now. Let's think about places we go, people we know, things we do. . . ."

"Are you ready to dig to find your buried stories? Okay, let's start remembering some things that have happened to you."

Marjorie circulates around the students on the rug, prompting students with the words from the chart or to use the chart.

- Guide children to use the chart at this time so they will use it when they are working independently.

In a whisper voice Marjorie brings the children back to her.

"Writers, let's come back together. Wow, I heard you dig up so many stories. Jennifer remembered one time she was at the park and she turned the slide into a water slide by pouring a bucket of water down the slide and then zipped down really fast. And Lillian thought of the first time she met Sam and how they became best friends!

"So writers, we are going to go off and write our stories so we can share them with each other. And remember, one way we can find where our stories are buried is to think about places we go, people we know, and things we do all the time. That's one way you can dig up the stories that happened to you."

- Point to the chart as you say this to remind students it is all on the chart.

"And don't forget, when you go off to write your stories you can draw first to help you remember, then write, write, write!

"Where are our stories buried? In the places we go, people we know, and things we do. All we have to do is be like Harry and dig, dig, dig! Off you go!"

As children move to their seats, Marjorie moves this chart to the bulletin board where the other writing charts are hanging.

- Keep the chart near you as you teach.
- Move the chart to where students can independently use it when writing.

Next Steps:

As the unit progresses, the teacher might add more strategies to the chart and invite the children to interact more and more with the chart. They can come up and point to strategies that have worked for them or add new strategies they discovered. Children can put their names on sticky notes and put the notes next to the strategy they used that day, or photocopies of student writing that further illustrates how the children are using the strategies could be added to the chart. The possibilities are endless, but the key thing to remember is that the charts need to be accessible to each child in your class. Constructing the charts in front of the students and using language and vocabulary that they can understand will help ensure readability and accessibility.

CHARTS IN ACTION

Use Icons, Drawings, and Color as Shorthand for Text

Figure 1.8 A sign in Taipei, Taiwan.

Now we come to the most important of all topics, providing visuals! As we mentioned in the Introduction, visual literacy has been a part of our children's lives from birth. They have been raised in a world filled with icons and images. Visuals are meant to make the complex simple. They also aid in quickly imbedding meaning into the context of the moment. Kristine learned this firsthand on a recent trip to Taipei, Taiwan. Arriving in a country where the print is so different and there is no familiar context for understanding this language, she found herself relying gratefully upon any and all visuals that clearly presented meaningful information. Walking down the stairs, for example, she knew to tread lightly after seeing the very graphic sign of a person falling backward (Figure 1.8).

One of the inherent beauties of a workshop structure is its consistency. The structure does not change whether you are in first grade or fifth grade, whether you are teaching reading or writing. The language and terminology do not change. Children are introduced to revision in kindergarten and continue to use this term for the rest of their lives as writers. They learn to make predictions as five-year-olds and as ten-year-olds. This provides incredible power and allows for ongoing growth and increasing sophistication. Icons and symbols can go across grades and be just as powerful.

What Visuals Do I Use?

Icons are images that become standard and are used over and over again to mean the same thing. Icons connect an image to meaning in a way that becomes instant. You don't have to think long about what it means. Once learned, it becomes automatic. Stop signs, arrows, and a skull and crossbones are all universal images that communicate a great deal of information in a split second. They are understood regardless of culture or language spoken. In other words, they are universal. But just because icons are considered to be universal, it does not mean they do not need to be taught and learned. Although most children come into school knowing what the triangular play symbol means on a DVD player, there was certainly someone in their lives who modeled its repeated use while imbedding meaning and purpose for this simple triangle-shaped icon. See Figure 1.9.

A Few Symbols and Their Possible Meanings
for Use on Classroom Charts

 !	Idea Warning Watch out
 ?	Confused Question Information
 ↻	Reread Look back Repeat
 (thought bubble)	Think Plan Remember
 ✳	Look Start here Important
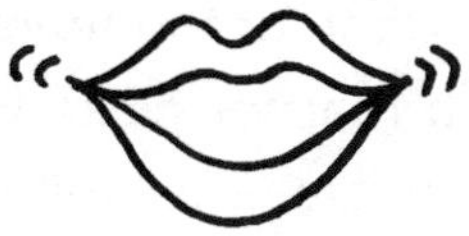 (mouth)	Speak Talk Say
 (eye)	Look Watch See
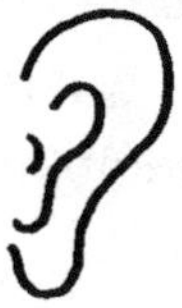 (ear)	Listen Hear

Figure 1.9

In the chart in Figure 1.1, the pencil is an icon that stands for writing. The power of the icon comes from the very real usage of a pencil or pen each and every day of a writers' workshop. Even if a young writer is unsure of what the words say, the pencil assures him that this chart is about writing. When the pencil appears on each and every writing chart, young writers learn to quickly spot the icon as a sign that this chart will help during writing time.

A thought bubble is another symbol used in the chart. This icon indicates that you are thinking even though the word *think* does not appear on the chart. The meaning of the chart would be significantly different if another popular symbol, the speech bubble, was employed. The thinking bubble lets the writer know that this is work you do in your head, on your own. A speech bubble would suggest this is work you do aloud, perhaps talking with a partner. The thought bubble, like the speech bubble, is an icon that writers become familiar with through reading and through their own work as writers, so the message is clear.

As with these examples, teachers can and should capitalize on well-known icons, as well as invent their own. One image we often use is a picture of a mouth. We use this image to mean one thing: *speak*. We use a picture of an eye to mean *look*. A picture of an ear means *listen*. You can find a way to draw these icons quickly by practicing using the least amount of lines as possible while still being recognizable. A mouth begins with two stretched out *m*'s. An ear begins as a question mark (?). Another great source is the computer. Many clip art images are available for free through the Internet. This does require some preplanning and cannot be used as easily on the spot. Some teachers print the icons on labels and peel them off when needed.

Drawing is another useful tool for the teacher to draw upon (no pun intended!). As soon as a teacher picks up a marker, children definitely become more attentive as they follow each stroke of the pen. One big advantage of drawing in front of children is that you can orally add to the meaning as you visually create the chart.

But How Do I Draw That?!

"But I can't draw!" Many people feel they can't draw. How many times have you or a friend said, "I can't draw a straight line with a ruler"? Have no fear. That is actually the first suggestion. Don't be afraid of what the final product will look like. It is actually more accessible if the end result resembles something your children could recreate themselves. Besides, most children think anything their teacher produces is beautiful.

It should also be simple. Start by drawing with shapes first. Several years ago, a group of art teachers visited the Teachers College Reading and Writing Project at Columbia University. They were quite stern with us regarding the stick figures we were drawing in front of children. "Any child who draws stick figures has learned that from an adult," they cautioned. They further explained that no child would ever developmentally come up with something like stick figures on his or her own. Children progress developmentally by drawing shapes and curved squiggles. Often that first shape is a circle. Many of our colleagues were stunned and a bit panicked, proclaiming, "But I can't draw!"

One of the art teachers replied calmly, "Yes, you can draw." Then she proceeded to show us staff developers how to use simple shapes to create any image from a person, to a dog, to a house, to an airplane, to a bike. It all comes down to seeing the world as a series of shapes. If you can make a circle, an oval, a rectangle, and a triangle, you too can draw. Think about a pencil, a drawing you will probably make for a writing chart: it is really made up of a long rectangle, a small square on top, and a triangle at the bottom (Figure 1.10).

Imagine you want to add a person to the chart in Figure 1.11. Circle at the top, circle or oval through the middle, and sticks for arms and legs. Eyelashes are not required to communicate the idea that you are talking about a person. Do not worry about perspective or shading; rather, make the drawing as simple as possible. Just like the idea that the language on a chart should only communicate the essentials, the same is true for visuals.

Simple, right?

Do not feel like you have to draw the writing booklet on the desk, a tile floor, and a fully dressed student in a chair, if all you really need to show is the booklet. All of the drawings above, from the pencil to the people, are nothing more than a series of lines and shapes. Visuals are a way to communicate a great deal of information quickly, while also making

Figure 1.10 Steps to draw a pencil.

Figure 1.11 Steps to draw a person.

that information memorable. Even visuals created by the shyest of artists make valuable meaning for our children. You can find more chart visuals in Appendix F.

What About Color?

Color can be used to beautify, but color can also be used to emphasize, distinguish, and complement the intended message. Most people don't need a Master of Fine Art degree to know that color can impact the senses and the soul. Whether choosing house paint or a new outfit, most of us know that color can affect mood, tone, and the initial impression one leaves on others. As teachers, we also know that color matters. Teachers probably buy more crayons and watercolor markers than children and their parents ever do.

Color has long been a tool used by teachers. Teachers understand the power of color-coding as an organizational method. The red folders are for math, the yellow folders are for writing, the blue folders are for reading. We color-code the vowels to distinguish them from the consonants. We color-code onsets and rimes. In dual-language classrooms, we distinguish each language by making everything in one language blue, the other language red. But designers also understand the importance color plays in the world of advertising and try to limit the amount of colors used to no more than five for cognitive clarity. They also know that a certain percentage of the population is color-blind, which is why black remains a favorite choice for ultimate impact.

When thinking about how to use color to support the messages we are trying to project in our charts, the key thing to place upfront and central is "purpose." *Purpose* implies outcomes and goals, as was discussed earlier, but it also takes into consideration scaffolds and supports. For example, if we want very young children to begin to internalize the difference between picture and print, then we might consider using color for the pictures and black only for the print, rather than making the vowels red in all the words. If we want to remind the students that every word usually has a vowel in it, then we might use red to highlight the presence of vowels in words. Contrast helps highlight differences and reinforces similarities.

Color can also create impact by its hue and tone (Figure 1.12). Pastels can be soothing, primary colors stimulating. Fluorescent colors provide a jolt. If you want to grab someone's attention, would you wave a lavender flag or a fluorescent orange flag? As teachers, we often want to grab students' attention. Therefore, it would make sense to use the colors that advertisers have long used to capture an unwitting public: Fluorescent colors. Fluorescent signs are meant to stop us in our tracks. Fluorescent signs are meant to warn us to stay clear. Fluorescent signs are meant to guide us toward the ultimate bargain. They are bold, they provide contrast, and they catch the average eye. Fluorescent rocks!

Fortunately, the world of office and school suppliers also knows this fact. We can find everything from sticky notes to index cards to folders to chart paper being produced in primary and fluorescent colors. On the one hand, we can be skeptical and suspect, but ultimately we know it to be a truth. Bright colors draw our attention. Bright colors are a way to draw attention to what we want our children to attend to. We can use this to be an effective tool in our classroom. When we make strategies on a chart in different colors, it helps children see that there is more than one option to help them reach a goal. Additionally, different colors allow teachers to help children isolate the needed information. Instead of trying to describe the visual or reread the words to the child, a teacher can quickly prompt, "Look at the yellow strategy on the 'Teach More' chart, that will help remind you to give examples." Color matters and how we use it matters.

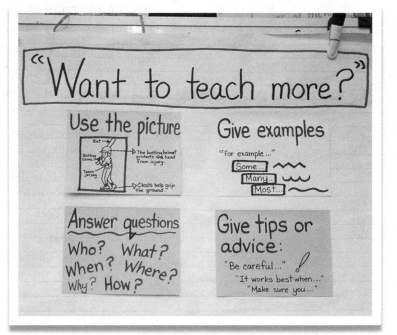

Fig. 1.12 "Want to Teach More?" chart (see inside back cover).

Using Student Work and Photographs of Students

Another compelling visual to consider is the students themselves. Putting photos of students up on your charts or examples of the work they produce definitely gets them to pay attention to the chart they star upon. All vanity aside, most of us pay closer attention when there is a chance we will see a photo of ourselves or a sample of our work whether in a scrapbook, or in a video, or tagged on Facebook. Kids are no different. In fact, they are eager to perform and produce when told you need some examples to put up on a chart. Photographing children in the act of doing each of the steps on a procedural chart, for example, encourages them to practice the skill and then provides an excellent visual model of each step involved. One popular chart created by many teachers at the beginning of the year shows the steps involved in coming to the meeting area. One photo shows a child pushing in her chair, the second photo is the child walking to the meeting area, and the third photo captures the child sitting "crisscross, applesauce" ready to begin. The chart in Figure 1.13 shows photographs of students engaged in appropriate conversational behaviors, which serves as a visual prompt of what "book talks" should look like throughout the day.

Hanging children's work up on charts also has a powerful effect on making charts an integral part of the classroom community. Using exemplars from published authors is an effective way teachers often show examples of writing craft on classroom charts. But when an example of a child's piece of writing is displayed alongside that of the pros, the whole class seems to sit a little taller and feel a bit prouder of what has been accomplished. It might be nice the way Donald Crews begins *Bigmama's* with dialogue, "Is it her? Is it Bigmama?" But when Dylan's new lead is hung up, "Is it the day yet? Is it the day for the tournament to begin?" the chart becomes truly memorable and owned by all.

Figure 1.13 Chart with photos of children from the classroom.

CHARTS IN ACTION: VISUALS ON CHARTS HELP STUDENTS RECALL AND RELIVE THE TEACHING FOCUS

Much of what teachers try to reinforce are routines and habits essential to both readers and writers as they progress across their day, week, and life so they come to know what it feels like to be productive readers and writers in the world. Earlier, we saw how one teacher helped her young writers generate topics for writing true stories from their lives and how a strategy chart was developed to reinforce the lesson and have as a reminder in case anyone got stuck. That example showed how charts can be used to support whole-class lessons. But what happens when a teacher has taught a series of lessons using a chart to support and reinforce the teaching and some children still don't seem to be using the strategies or procedures taught or the chart as a helpful reminder?

The following transcript recounts an episode a teacher, Ms. Geoffrey, had with a group of first and second graders gathered together for the shared purpose of using a set of procedures to make for a productive use of the writing workshop time. The routines for planning one's writing time had been taught with several steps to help writers begin work on their writing immediately. This group of children needed additional help in setting themselves up for a productive workshop despite the lessons taught. This particular group needed more practice for the behavior to become a habit. There was a routines chart already created and hanging in the classroom showing the steps of preparing for writing time, but it was not being referred to or used by this particular group of children. The short-term goal was to get the children to use this routines chart to help them become more productive from the opening moments of writers' workshop, but the ultimate goal is for the behaviors to become internalized and for the chart to be no longer needed.

Lesson Focus: We set ourselves up before the lesson to make sure we have a strong day of writing.

Materials:

- **Student writing folders**
- **Chart, "How to Set Up for Writers' Workshop" with photographs of the children (see Figure 1.14)**

"Guess what? I've noticed that both of you are so strong at using our charts to help you get ideas for writing. I noticed that you often walk over to that chart and use it to help you get started for writing. That is so smart and strong of you! Did you realize what independent writers you have become?"

Sam shrugs. Thalia nods.

"Today I wanted to remind you that strong independent writers get themselves ready to make the most out of their writing time. Sometimes we need a tool to help us remember what to do, and the charts in our room can be really useful tools to help us remember how to do things."

Chart Tips:

- Refer to the charts as tools and celebrate their use. This will lead to increased independence and confidence.

Sam points and says, **"Yeah, sometimes I use that chart over there to remind me what to do when I'm done with my writing."**

"There is another writing chart right near that one that helps us set up for a serious day of writing. Can you find it?

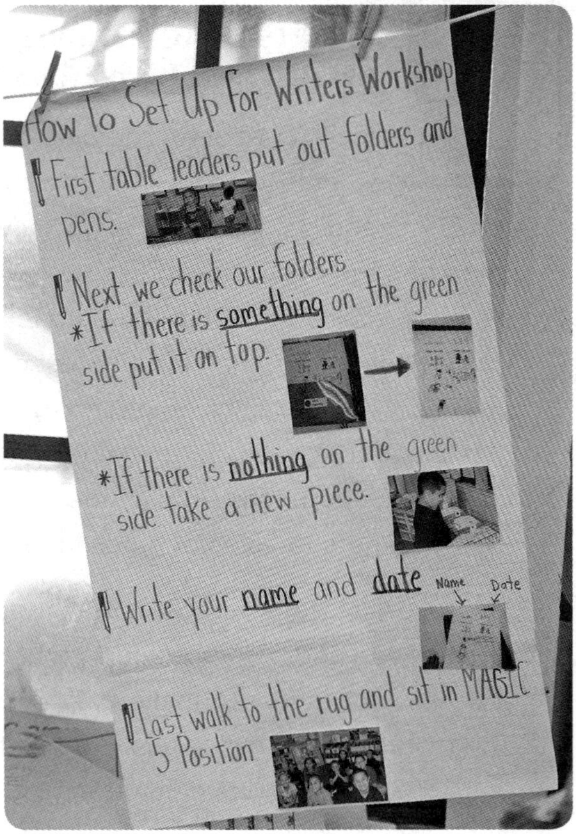

Figure 1.14 *"Writers' Workshop"* routine chart.

The students start pointing at the clothesline. **"That one!"** Thalia yells.

- Use clear headings and visuals so that children can distinguish charts at a glance.
- Cluster charts together by subject or topic so that children can find them quickly.

Ms. Geoffrey unclips the chart "How to Set Up for Writers' Workshop" from the clothesline in front of the windows and brings it to the eye level of the small group.

- Have charts at a level that is easy to reach and read.
- Use a clip system so you can easily move the chart to where it is needed.

"I took pictures so that you can check the chart and remember how your bodies should look like the pictures to make sure you did each step of the set-up routine."

Sam points to the third step and announces, **"That's me!"**

- Take pictures of the child approximating a skill, as opposed to the child who has mastered it, because the photo will be a constant prompt to do it again!

"So let's try that here together. Let's use the pictures to get us ready for workshop. Look at the first one. Sam, what's happening in the first picture?"

■ Use the photos to help children recall the teaching.

Sam says, **"The folders are at the table."**

"Great! Did that happen?"

Both children look to the table and nod.

"Okay, go grab them and meet me back here by the time I count down from five."

Ms. Geoffrey begins counting and Sam and Thalia quickly get their folders and return to the rug.

"Thalia, step two, look at the picture, what's happening?"

Thalia studies the photo for a minute.

"Look on the green side? And take it out?"

Ms. Geoffrey nods. Both students open their folders and look at the green and red sides. Both students have several unfinished writing booklets on the green side. Sam grabs one and puts it on his folder. Thalia pauses and Ms. Geoffrey leans in and whispers, *"Choose one."* Thalia grabs the top one and puts it on top.

Ms. Geoffrey looks at Sam and just taps the next photo.

■ Move to nonverbal cueing so that children are using the chart more independently.

Sam says **"Get paper!"** and starts to get up.

Thalia stops him.

"No!" Thalia says, **"We don't need it, we have a story."**

Sam sits back down. Wordlessly, Ms. Geoffrey taps the next photo.

"Name and date," the children say together and glance down. Thalia puts her finger on her name and then the date as Sam writes the date. Both students look back up at the chart and say, **"Go to the rug!"**

■ Provide students with repeated practice of using the photos to enable students to move toward independence.

Thalia smiles, **"We are already on the rug!"**

CHARTS IN ACTION

"See how the chart helped us get ready for a great day of writing? We realized we had stories we could go back to, added names and dates when we forgot, and are ready for new teaching! The pictures are here to help you make sure you do each and every step. Let's use the photos one more time to help us remember how to set up for writers' workshop."

Ms. Geoffrey taps the pictures and Thalia and Sam say each step.

■ Pictures allow children to describe the step even if they can't read the writing on the chart.

"Every time you write you can use this chart to help you set up. Now let's go hang it back up together so you will always know where to look."

Next Steps:

The teacher may decide to make a smaller version of the chart to be used individually if she sees any of the children needing a more immediate and hands-on reminder of the strategy in question. The smaller version can be put in each child's folder or added to a table tent and placed on their table during writing time. First, observe from afar, then up close, to assess how each child is doing and determine some next steps that will help habitualize the behaviors we hope each child internalizes and ultimately owns.

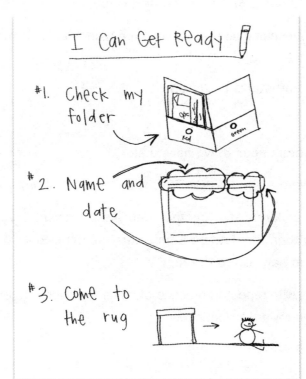

Charts can be simplified for easy, independent use.

Last Words

Catchy clear headings will bring your readers and writers to the charts and help them identify the ones that will be most helpful for their current work. Direct, explicit, and readable language will support young readers and writers in identifying the strategy or step they need support with, and simple purposeful visuals will quickly allow each student to recall far more than the words encapsulate. This will not come easily at first, but through trial and error you will find the few words and pictures that work for complex and abstract teaching. Your charts serve as reminders of teaching, not the teaching itself, just like the sticky note on your dashboard that says, "Pick up dog food." "Use talking" will bring children back to the lesson, the demonstration, and the bigger work you have taught. Colleagues are an essential ingredient in the paring down of language and creation of visuals. Come together and challenge each other: write it in fewer words, draw it faster, come up with a catchier heading. Two heads will always be better than one when creating charts. With all things, there is never perfection, only possibility. When one version doesn't work, try another, and another. Innovate and elaborate and explore. The next section will help you identify ways to engage children in the chart-making process and drive the usage and independence of your young readers and writers into another dimension.

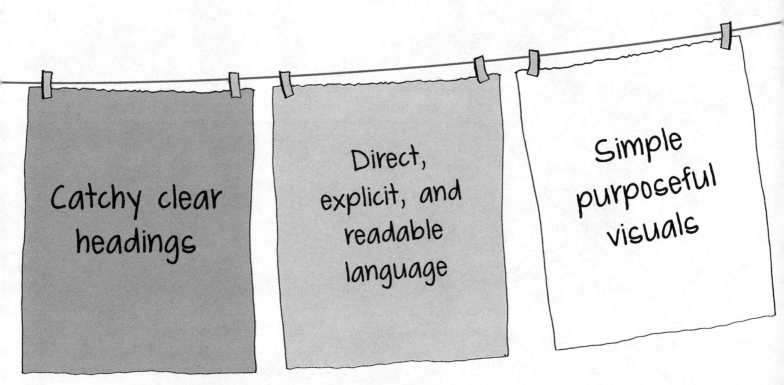

*Chart is at a level children can use.

*Sticky notes allow children to interact with charts.

Section 2

How Can I Help My Students Use the Charts Independently?

Figure 2.1 A student interacts with a strategy chart.

Do visitors to your classroom *ooh* and *ahh* over the charts hanging in your classroom? Do they pull out their phones to take pictures of your chart art? Do they compliment you on your charts' clarity and color? It feels good, right? But when they leave do you find yourself looking around at your students wondering, "Why do they come to me for help instead of going to one of the charts?" The nagging question lingers, "Why don't they *use* any of these amazing charts?" Well, in this section we provide several suggestions to answer this universal lament.

In this section we talk about when and how to make charts with students in ways that are both engaging and efficient because we know how critical time management is for most teachers. Then we give lots of tips for making your charts accessible even when wall space is at a minimum. Finally, we show how to bring charts to life using music, chants, and rhymes that truly make charts memorable and fun for all your students.

At this point, you have more than a few chart-making fundamentals under your belt, things that commercial chart makers and advertisers have known for years. However, creating beautiful charts will not in itself make for more independent students; this involves the teaching you do while using the charts. So let's take the great work you've done creating visually exciting, meaningful charts a step further.

In this section, we'll talk about physically making charts that promote independent student use (Figure 2.1). Practical suggestions will also be included for efficient chart making, along with strategies for making charts accessible and a close look at a chart-making session that explores how you can make a chart with children, not just for them. In addition, several solutions will be offered for the typical challenges teachers face with charts, including location and making charts memorable through shared reading, song and rhyme, as well as reading and writing connections.

Making Charts with Students, or with Students in Mind

As we mentioned in the Introduction, ready-made charts can be enticing as they are colorful, shiny, perfection personified. And they are easy—just hang up and voila! Done. This ease of use can lead to charts quickly wallpapering every corner of your classroom. And, because we have spent many hard-earned dollars on these charts, we often want to get our money's worth by giving them permanent spots in the classroom. The result is charts hung more for decoration than for any clearly targeted instructional purpose. Unless we make a conscious effort to construct the charts in front of the children and with the children, they will simply become part of the decor, a backdrop to the actions going on between the teacher and the students. For this reason, charts are rarely premade and just hung up like a fine art print on a gallery wall.

Have you ever walked into the main office, gathered your mail from your mailbox, headed into your classroom, and then later that day find yourself shocked by a fire drill? As you gathered outside with your colleagues, you expressed surprise that no one let the teachers know this would happen, and among murmurs of agreement, someone said, "There was a sign above the time clock."

Sure enough, when you went back to the office later that day, above the time clock, among a cacophony of notes, hung a sign: "Fire Drill at 1 PM." Unless a fuss is made, or we are part of the creation, changes in our environment can often go unnoticed. Like a sign in the office, a new picture in the hallway, or even sometimes a new building on the block, we can be oblivious to the world around us unless there is something to distinguish the change or someone draws our attention to it, waking us up from our revelry, making us conscious of what is new to our environment.

This line of thought underscores the critical importance of students actively creating and participating in chart making in the classroom with the teacher. "But," you may ask, "When in the day? Won't that take forever? What if I like it to be perfect and I can't do that quickly?" Step one: Take a deep breath. Now let's take these worries one question at a time.

When Should I Make Charts with Students?

The easy answer here is: It depends. You might make a chart with students at the beginning of a lesson so that they can refer back to it throughout their time working independently. You could also wait until the end of a lesson to make a chart, using it to wrap up and solidify the work of the day. You could stop a lesson in the middle and take a few minutes to make a chart to help students get back on track. It could happen for five minutes at the end of the school day, or for ten minutes of interactive writing time. The question to ask yourself is, "When would it make sense to make this chart?" If something is complex and multistep, like using reasons to support an opinion, you might make that chart with students before the lesson, but if the teaching is more inquiry based, for example, exploring ways readers can work with partners, you might wait until the end of the workshop to see what ways children worked together, what they tried, and add that onto the chart. If you are making a heading for a chart, or perhaps writing a "How to Shop for Books" chart, that creation could happen at any time of the day and can be referenced later when needed during reading or writing time.

But Won't That Take Forever? Ideas for Efficient Chart Making

You might be thinking, "It takes me twenty minutes to make a chart; that seems like a long time to hold kids on the rug." You are right, it is, but streamlining the process can make a world of difference in both time and impact. First a reminder, you will rarely sit down to make a whole chart with children at one time, because charts record a series of teaching over time. At most you are adding a bullet point of information on to the chart; sometimes that bullet point might have a few steps to it, but never should it be a paragraph of information (see "Knowing Your Students Makes for More Efficient Charting" table on the following page). Once you know what part you are adding to the chart, you have to decide: "What will I make in front of and with the students?" and "What will I have prepared ahead of time?" Consider a cooking show. When a chef sets out to show viewers how to make a dish, some items have been set up ahead of time. Perhaps the carrots, onions, and celery are already cut and measured in a bowl, and the oil may already be simmering in the pan. The chef does this because he or she only has a set amount of time, and this isn't a show about how to chop vegetables. However, when the chef is teaching the tricky part of the meal, like the trimming and sautéing of the meat (also the most expensive part of the meal), the chef will slow down and show that piece of the puzzle step-by-step. In this same way, our teaching with charts will have some prep work done ahead of time, and the part that we want children to hang on to is slowed down and highlighted. (See Figure 2.2.)

Figure 2.2 A teacher, Ms. Siotkas, uses a large, premade sticky note to teach a small group.

Knowing Your Students Makes for More Efficient Charting

If You Know . . .	Then You Might . . .
This is a new skill or topic for your children.	Make the heading together during a shared writing experience (like interactive writing or shared writing).
This is a familiar skill to your children.	Prewrite the heading and reread it quickly with your students.
Your children are beginning readers or writers.	Draw the icon or place the visual during the lesson using gestures to reinforce the meaning of the pictures. If you haven't prewritten the words already, quickly write the words in front of the students.
Your children may not know the vocabulary you are planning to use.	Generate the language for the chart with the children and write it with the class. You can add visuals quickly in the moment or add them later on.
This chart is more of a review.	Put three or four bullets on the chart at one time. The writing and visuals may be predone and revealed to the students throughout the lesson, which gives them choices.

Anticipated situations with possible solutions

Let's unpack this chart a bit. If this is a new skill or topic for the children, for example, imagine a reading chart on tricky words, you could make the heading ahead of time or you could make it with your students. If it is an entirely new concept, and you want the readers in the room to have repeated exposure to the concept, you might make the heading with the students during interactive writing (see the following Charts in Action section). On the other hand, if this is a familiar skill and your second graders have been figuring out tricky words for years now, you probably just need to jog their memory. In that case, premaking the heading and reading it together will be enough support. Because the heading is never the whole point of a lesson, you don't want to take time away from the "meat" of your teaching. Either way, by the time you get to the focus of the lesson, the chart will have a heading that underscores and emphasizes the teaching point, like "Tricky Words Won't Stop Us!"

Then you can move on to teaching some actual strategies for solving tricky words. You might be teaching that one way to solve tricky words is to use what is happening in the story and the picture, then look at the first part of the hard word, imagining what would make sense. You have to decide exactly how much of this to create in front of the students. Once again, time and understanding of the students' prior knowledge are considerations. You could decide to prewrite the words on the chart and make the icons in front of the students if you know they are beginning readers or writers and the icons are what they will reference again and again. In that case, you will want their input on what to draw to represent each step of the strategy, so they will better understand what each part means. For this reason you might come prepared with a large sticky note that says:

- What's happening?
- Look at the first chunk.
- What makes sense?

Then together with the students, decide what visual will help remember each part of the strategy. Quickly draw in a visual next to each phrase, as you say each phrase again. You could even have the children draw the visual in the air and say the phrase as well. The more styles of learning incorporated, the more likely students will be to remember what is on the chart and why.

On the flip side, if the children are unlikely to know the vocabulary you are planning to use, the icons can be prepared ahead of time, or you could use student work or photos gathered the day before, but in either case you want to use the language of your students to describe the how. You might then have some icons drawn on large sticky notes and ask, "How should we say this?" then add the words the students use to describe each step of the strategy. The key is not trying to do everything at once. Some of the chart is prepared ahead of time (when time and aesthetics are an issue), and some is built with the students, but the whole focus of the lesson is captured and discussed with students and can be referred back to or added to as needed.

Finally, there may be times the chart you are using is more of a review of strategies previously taught (either earlier in the

year or during the prior grade level). In this case, the writing and visuals can be done ahead of time and revealed to the students as the lesson progresses, one at a time for emphasis, showcasing a repertoire of strategies children have to draw upon. This works particularly well when you want to empower children to be active problem solvers and decision makers when it comes to helping themselves move forward when stuck. For example, if you have taught, or know that the previous teachers have taught, three key elements for elaborating a story (action, dialogue, and feelings), then prepare the heading and each illustrated bullet ahead of time. Then, as you remind the children of each strategy they know, slap each one up on the chart, emphasizing the fact that they know these. Then sweep your hand grandly over the strategies and say, "So writers, you have some decisions to make about how you are going to elaborate your stories. You need to think about which strategies you use the most, which ones you use sometimes, and which strategies you hardly ever use." Then invite the children to look over their stories and look over the chart to make plans for how they can make their stories grow. This type of chart can also easily be made into individual checklists for children to keep close to them as reminders of the choices they have to help themselves.

But What If I Am a Perfectionist? Making the Best Chart in the Least Amount of Time

Welcome to the club! One of the things teachers often struggle with in the classroom is the sometimes mutually exclusive need for neatness and in-the-moment student engagement. And neatness does matter! Your writing serves as a model and a mentor for your students, and clarity is key to students using the charts again and again. So what to do? Here are two options, though you certainly have even more.

- The first option is to use a small dry erase board or the SMART Board to capture the ideas for icons or language and roughly sketch out that part of the chart with students. Then later, neatly recreate what you decided upon as a class on the permanent paper chart. Keep the language and icons the same as on the sketch you did together and review it with the students once it is on the public chart.

● The second option resides with some available tools. They are *big* (6 × 8 inch) sticky notes or the restickable glue stick that turns any piece of paper into a sticky note. (Scotch has one, as does Elmer's, but they call it "repositionable." We will wait here as you go order it and the big sticky notes online.) The headings go on the big chart paper, but the different teaching foci go on the sticky notes, or any 8½ × 11-inch page you make into a sticky note. That way, if something goes awry as you are making it, you only need to recreate a sticky note, not the whole chart. These large sticky notes or repositionable glue sticks also make charts instantly more accessible for students, which will be discussed in more detail next.

CHARTS IN ACTION: CO-CREATING CHARTS WITH STUDENTS

The following session took place in a first-grade classroom in November during an interactive writing session. In this classroom, the teacher does ten to fifteen minutes of interactive writing daily. Together the class composes and writes stories, letters, lists, signs, and, many times, charts. In this school, students have worked with partners in reading in kindergarten and also during read-aloud time, so the students are familiar with ways to work with partners. The purpose for the chart being created on this day is to review these behaviors and then create an exemplar chart with photographs of the children modeling the ways partners can work together. This will give the children a clear vision for how partnerships should look during workshop time.

Lesson Focus: Ways to Work with Reading Partners

Materials:

- Four pieces of colored paper made into sticky notes with the repositionable glue stick
- A white piece of chart paper that already says "What Can Partners Do?"
- Whiteboards and dry erase markers for each student
- Sticky notes or white cover-up tape
- Black magic marker

Ms. Wotman begins her interactive writing session.

"First graders, we have been working so very hard at our reading, and I was thinking about how tomorrow we should learn more about how we can work with our partners. But then I thought, Hey! These first graders already know a lot about working with partners in reading because you've had partners since September. In fact, you've had reading partners since kindergarten. Right?"

Choruses of **"Yeah! Yeah we do!"** Alyssa's voice drowns out a few others saying, **"Yeah and in kindergarten me and my partner were the Billy Goats, trip trap, trip trap."** Alyssa begins slapping the ground with her hands acting like the Billy Goat and is quickly joined by other students.

"Yes, I knew it! I knew you knew about things like acting out! So can you now turn and talk to your partner and tell them some of the things that you know to do with a reading partner, so we can make a chart to use during our reading time?"

Chart Tips

- Establish a purpose for the chart-related writing. In this case, they will be making a chart about reading partnerships.

- Invite students in on the process of capturing shared knowledge and placing it on a chart.

As students turn and talk, Alyssa continues to embellish on the infamous Billy Goats Gruff saying, **"And we made the bridge, and I was the troll and my partner said trip, trap, trip, trap, and I said . . ."** Meanwhile, Galiliea and Gilbert are quietly saying, **"We read it together."** The teacher leans in and asks, *"Like the same book at the same time?"* and they nod. Joey turns to Mihal and says, **"We said this is the same and this is the same."** Ms. Wotman leans in and says, *"Oh, you talked about some parts?"*

- Listen for the type of language the children use to express their thinking so the writing you do on the chart is similar.

- Restate and use more specific language to introduce vocabulary that will help students express what they know in clear terms.

"Okay, one, two, three, look at all these eyes on me! So I heard three big things. I heard that partners can read together, talk together, and act it out."

The teacher holds up a finger for each one.

"Do you see that? Can you say back those three things to your partner?"

Students turn and say back the three things.

- Have children repeat the key points so that they are actively participating in chart creation. This will also help with memory. (All this happens in a matter of seconds, not minutes.)

"Okay, so I think we might be ready to add this to our chart. This will be such a huge help when partner time comes and we aren't sure what to do!

"Okay, so let's read the heading again."

- State the purpose for the chart and when it might come in handy.

Everyone reads as Ms. Wotman points, her voice louder than the rest: *"What can partners do?"*

- Engage children in shared reading of the heading to ensure that even those who are emergent readers will know what these bolded words say.

"Okay, the first thing we said was, 'We read together!' Okay, as I say it, I want you to count the words: 'We . . . read . . . together.' How many words?"

Choruses of **"Three! Three!"**

"Okay, so I am going to draw three lines on this bright yellow paper so it is really clear that there are three words. That will make our chart easier to read. Say the words as I draw the lines: **We. Read. Together.**

"Okay, so who can help us with this first word, we. *It's a snap word that is up on our word wall, but I bet you don't even need to look on the word wall because you can spell it in a snap!"*

■ Use a different color to clarify and make each strategy separate and unique.

■ Reinforce the purpose for the chart and the accessibility of the chart.

The children nod and glance quickly at the word wall to confirm. Then Ms. Wotman gestures for a student to come up. (See Figure 2.3.)

■ Create a situation in which children feel connected to the chart because they have helped make it.

"Did you find we? *This is where we are going to write it. As Keyana writes it here, you can write it on your whiteboard."*

Children begin to wave around whiteboards with the word *we* (some uppercase, some lowercase). Keyana has written *we* on the paper.

Figure 2.3 When mistakes happen, fix-ups are fast and fun.

"Okay, lets reread: **We.** *It's really important that we can all read the words on a chart so we know what to do if we forget!*

"What was the next word? **Read!** *Oh, that's a turtle word, say it slow and write the sounds you hear on your board! Julissa, come write it, and everyone else, once you think you have it, show it!*

"Okay, lets read it. 'We read . . . .'"

- Reinforce the purpose for the chart and remind the children how they can use it to help themselves independently.

- Engage in multiple readings so that the content of the chart is known to all children regardless of reading level.

Students say, **"Together!"** Joey chimes in, **"That's a hard word!"**

"Okay, I am going to write it, watch how I think about it in parts."

Teacher models thinking about the parts in *together* while the students are working the word out on their own whiteboards.

"Okay, lets reread the whole chart so far. 'What can partners do? We read together.'"

The teacher repeats the process for "We talk together," but after writing that, the first graders are getting antsy. The teacher decides to quickly write "Act it out," then everyone rereads the whole chart. (See Figure 2.4.)

"Fantastic. And you know what I am thinking would make this chart even better? Pictures! We can take photographs during reading workshop of different partnerships doing these three things and then hang them next to our words. That will help everyone remember what reading partners can do when they get together and see exactly what it should look like.

Figure 2.4 The rest of the class participates by writing the chart words on whiteboards.

- Encourage students to try out the strategies and become teaching stars in the classroom by announcing that photos will be taken of those using these strategies, to be placed on the chart later.

- Insert photographs later as a supportive concrete visual.

"Okay, friends, before we end for the day, we want to put this chart somewhere we can see it, because this is really going to help partners work together. Let's see, hmm, there is lots of space right next to our 'Getting Ready to Read' chart. Let's put it there! Ready, follow me with your eyes as I put it up. Friends, just like you look at the schedule when you want to see what we are going to do today, you can look here when you want to know what to do with your reading partner. Can you turn and tell your partner one more time what this chart says?"

- Involve children in the decision-making process and lay the foundation for the chart-filled year ahead by discussing where in the room the chart should be hung up.

Next Steps:

When reading time comes along, this chart can be referred to during the lesson or revised, adding new ways partners can work together, or you might take off "talk together" and replace it with more specific ways to talk about books as the children develop and grow. The chart could also be illustrated with photographs of partnerships taken during the reading workshop. Hand-drawn pictures or clip art can also visually show the different ways partners can work together during reading time. Making charts with students, not just for students, hands over ownership and empowers all members of the classroom community to be active and engaged learners.

Making Charts Accessible and Adaptable

As you have been reading, a niggling question might be growing louder: "But where do I put all of these charts?" Because charts work as anchors for students and provide opportunities for independent problem solving, they must be visible for the students when they are needed. There are a range of options, whether you have lots of wall space or are stymied by strict fire code regulations.

Classrooms with Multiple Spaces for Charts

Sometimes many posted charts can be its own problem, overwhelming students with too much print so that it becomes difficult for young readers and writers to use charts independently. (Remember the fire drill note obscured by the sheer number of notes surrounding it?) To tackle this, consider giving each board a theme: reading, writing, math, science, and so on. At the beginning of the year, commit space for specific charts to hang on each board. That means each space will stay empty until you have begun making charts. That is okay! You will only need to save space for about three or four charts, because it is unlikely you will have more than four goals to conquer in a unit (see Section 1 on creating charts using goals). This may seem like a lot of space, but some charts may not be full size, and others will be incorporating student work and student images. To make sure you do not fill in the space ahead of time, hang a few pieces of blank chart paper, as placeholders, and alert students, "We are going to be filling up these pages with all of our learning!" (See Figure 2.5.)

Figure 2.5 Clotheslines can provide additional space.

Figure 2.6 Current charts are grouped together on a bulletin board.

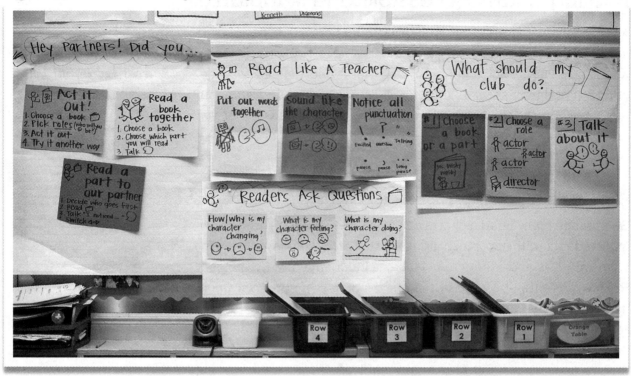

Also try to make sure writing charts are near writing materials, reading charts near reading materials, and so on (Figure 2.6.). Keeping the space consistent year-round assures students know exactly where to look when they have questions about reading or writing. Some teachers keep reading and writing charts near each other so they can make connections between the two. To reinforce the location, you can hold small groups by the charts needed for the lesson or send children to the space to find what they need on their own. The prime space should be for current instructional charts and have places for charts to retire to, but more on that later.

Classrooms with One Bulletin Board

If you do not have the space to have all charts out at all times, there are still ways to make sure charts are accessible when they are needed (see Figure 2.7). It is useful to allot a space on the board for several charts, but you can also affix clips or hooks over each of the spaces so this space becomes a rotating area where subject-specific charts are hung at the time needed. To hold the charts not in use, you might cluster them using a clothing rack or a five-skirt hanger. For example, one skirt hanger can hold three or four reading charts, another one can hold the writing charts, and one can hold the math charts that represent your current instructional work. As you transition from one subject to another, for example, a child could be responsible for taking down the math charts and hanging up the writing charts. To make this easier for young readers and writers to differentiate the subjects, you might color-code the charts. All the reading charts might be written in blue, the writing charts in purple, and so on. Or if you have multicolored chart paper, you could designate one color for each subject. Then once the subject is done, the charts are moved from their place on the board as the next needed charts are placed.

Figure 2.7 Charts can be hung together on skirt hangers until needed.

Classrooms with Restricted Wall Use

We have been in schools with incredibly stringent fire code regulations and teachers are prevented from hanging anything anywhere. If this is your situation, have hope, as there are several ways around this. One brilliant solution we learned from *Making Your Teaching Stick* by Shanna Schwartz (2008). Shanna suggests when short on space to create "table tents" by taping together a couple of simple file folders to create a self-standing form that can sit on each table (Figure 2.8). You then attach sheet protectors or clips on each side, and photocopied minicharts can slide into each sheet protector or be attached by clips. This allows for each side to hold a different chart. As you teach something new, you can give each table a small sticky note with the teaching focus to add to the chart where it belongs. These charts will still grow

Figure 2.8 Table tents bring the charts to the children.

Figure 2.9 A portable chart book makes it easy to bring charts to groups of children.

as the unit progresses, but rather than one large chart, several small charts will be growing simultaneously. You can also create a binder or folder for each subject to hold examples of current charts. These portable chart books become part of the materials that are put out prior to each reading or writing time (or other subject area).

If for some reason this does not work, you might then make several shared class chart books. (See Figure 2.9.) You can use one large, spiral sketch pad for each subject area that will need charts. (We find 11 × 14 inches or 16 × 20 inches to be a good size.) Make a tab for each unit, and as you make the charts, they stay in the sketch pad. When students need to access the charts, they can get up and flip through the book. Because you have each unit tabbed, it will not be too difficult for students to find what they need on their own. We discourage keeping all charts on one large flip chart. For starters, it is often too big and unwieldy for children to manage without help, and also, it is much harder to wade through all subjects to find the one chart needed. Several smaller, lighter chart books will keep your walls clear while still keeping the charts accessible for your students.

Make It Stick: Providing Up-Close Access to Charts

Several times now, large sticky notes and the repositionable glue stick have been mentioned as tools to help make charts. The real beauty of these tools, though, is how they allow static charts to become interactive and flexible. When parts of our charts are on sticky notes, those parts can travel. A student who is struggling with a certain step or strategy can walk up and claim the sticky note for that step or strategy and return back to his seat, aid in hand, to help with his work. Perhaps you have a small group of students who are struggling with giving stories a sense of closure; you could grab the sticky note that has the strategy to help with endings and bring it to those students to use in a small group. These tools allow the chart to move to students.

The opposite is also possible. Rather than asking students to take something from a chart, we can use sticky notes to ask them to add to the chart. We could ask students to write their name on a sticky note and add it to the chart they are planning to use that day. (See Figure 2.10.) Or we might ask children to add an example of the way they used a chart. If I am helping students add setting to their stories, we could photocopy a piece of student work and add that onto the chart with the re-positionable glue stick. Both of these two techniques—having students take part of the chart or add to the chart—increase children's interactions with these tools.

Making Charts Memorable: Using Music, Chanting, and Rhyme

"Plop, plop, fizz, fizz, oh what a relief it is." Or think back to the last wedding you attended and did the chicken dance, or "By Men-nen." Once a tune gets into your head, it often won't leave, even years after it originally entered through the ears and settled into your cerebral cortex. The eyes and the ears are two of the most powerful vehicles through which information enters our system, traveling through the brain, finding multiple places to lodge. It appears that even somewhat meaningless stimuli, like the previous jingle, can settle into long-term memory and be easily recalled if it is repeated often and has a rhythm or rhyme attached to the words. So setting information to a tune helps make things memorable. The most common example is the ABC song, twenty-six letters sung to the tune of "Twinkle, Twinkle, Little Star" (a tune by Mozart, by the way) that is learned by young children across the world (Wolfe 2001). When most children can only remember one or two bits of information at a time, how is it they can remember twenty-six letters? The only explanation is they first sing it as a

Figure 2.10 A teacher, Ms. Biggane, gives her children sticky notes to set goals.

song, then attach the rhythmic sounds to the visual letters and, voila! The alphabet is learned (with perhaps the exception of "L M N O P").

Teachers have long known the power of teaching through the use of tunes. Whether teaching multiplication tables (two, four, six, eight) or the parts of the body (heads, shoulders, knees, and toes), a tune helps children learn information. One reason for this phenomenon is music engages the emotions. Memories are often awoken when a certain song comes over the radio and quickly transports us back in time. Music can calm, energize, or cause goose bumps. Marjorie once met an actress who had recently received recognition for her role in a campy horror movie. When Marjorie asked her if it was scary being in a horror film, she smiled and said, "Not at all. It only becomes scary when they add the music." Marjorie never forgot that casual comment because in that moment she realized the actress was right. Try turning off the sound while watching "Night of the Living Dead" and you will know what she meant. Fear quickly turns to laughter, even groans.

Elementary school teachers also know that singing songs, chanting chants, and recalling rhymes is fun for all involved, and what is fun engages and delights children of all ages, which in turn, often extends the amount of time children want to participate in any given activity. And the more often an activity is repeated, the more likely it will be remembered. Give yourself a minute to recall the popular wedding song, the chicken dance, and almost involuntarily your arms start to flap and your hips start to wiggle, and a stupid grin comes to your face. Little more than repetition and an engaging environment have taught scores of us this complex dance. There is no better place to bring this knowledge of learning to bear than when creating charts in the classroom.

Charts, Chants, and Cheers

As mentioned earlier, charts advertise our teaching, and like advertisers and educators alike, we want the charts to be engaging, enjoyable, and memorable so our teaching really sticks. If you find, for example, children are not using a chart, or not using one bullet on a chart, you may do more to draw their attention to that chart or bullet. You may decide to include some kind of rally cry that raises the energy level of the students and gets them stoked to do what the chart, or bullet, is suggesting. For example, on a chart

about ways to elaborate your writing, Kristine found children were still not using actions. She looked again at what the bullet on the chart said: "Add actions to our writing. Ask, what did my body and my face do? Write it!" Although this summarized the content and clearly expressed what she wanted her young writers to do each and every time they wrote a story, the bullet was a bit ordinary, a bit dull, plus many of the children weren't actually adding actions to their stories. So she asked the children for their help.

Kristine began by saying, "I was reading over this chart and there is a lot of good information about ways to make our writing come to life, but the bullet about action doesn't seem to get used very much." She looked toward the chart with a puzzled look on her face, then turned back to the class and asked, "What might make a great rallying cry that would get more writers interested in trying this strategy?" The room erupted into chatter. As she listened into the many conversations going on, Kristine realized her students actually had lots of ideas that she had not considered. After sharing out the many ideas, the class chose one they thought would make a great rallying cry:

> *Action, action, is the way*
> *to make our writing come to life,*
> *each and every day.*
> *Yeah!*

Kristine wrote it down on the dry erase board, and they practiced reading it out loud to hear how it sounded. The class tried clapping, slapping, and tapping to see which phrase had the best beat. A word or two was changed and a couple more words were crossed out until the phrase had a smooth, rhythmic beat. Once everyone agreed it sounded good being shouted out loud, Kristine suggested everyone try whispering and snapping the chant as they went off to write. The effect was a little bit like a scene from West Side Story; "Action [*snap*], action [*snap*], is the way [*snap*] to bring our writing [*snap*] to life [*snap*] each day [*snap*]. Yeah! [*Clap!*]" Throughout the day, and longer, children could be heard whispering the chant, and more importantly, looking back at the chart about action. Inviting the children to create a rallying cry was a definite boost to both the energy and the interest in making this one chart come to life in the classroom and made her deeply aware of the power possible when teachers allow children to become co-creators of the curriculum.

Musical Moments Can Make Anything Memorable

Music is another major motivator teachers use to make teaching memorable. Besides putting the ABC song to the tune of "Twinkle, Twinkle, Little Star," there is not a single teachable moment that cannot be put to a tune of some kind or other. Marjorie's favorites tend to be the classics, like "Frère Jacques," "Row, Row, Row Your Boat," and "Mary Had a Little Lamb" (also put to a tune by Mozart). But many teachers have also used the toe-tapping, finger-snapping world of rap and other popular music to bring their instructional words to life. One way to do this is to consider each bullet on your chart and see if you can put it to a tune. One chart Marjorie tried this with was a procedural chart designed to remind children of the steps they could take to make their writing easier to read, both for themselves and for others. The three key points were: (1) Say the word. (2) Write the word. (3) Read the word.

She started by singing the words as they were written. Marjorie thought about what it was she really wanted children to remember. This led her to *"Don't forget to* say the word." Then she tried to get a tune in her head that these words could lay alongside. Marjorie started humming and realized the tune she was humming was "Mary Had a Little Lamb." What's great about getting a tune in your head is that you find you have to take away or add in extra words in order to match the beat and rhythm of the song in your head. This is the song Marjorie created to reinforce the bulleted points on this particular chart:

Writing Words We Can Read!
(to the tune of "Mary Had a Little Lamb")

Don't forget to
Say the word,
Say the word,
Say the word.
Don't forget to
Say the word,
Each and every
Time!

Every time you
Write a word,
Write a word,
Write a word,

*Every time you
Write a word,
Make sure you read it too!*

*Now everyone can
Read your book,
Read your book,
Read your book,
Now everyone can
Read your book,
Each and every
Page!*

Figure 2.11 A class sings the chart.

One other important thing Marjorie did was to use gestures to reinforce the words. So when she sang, "Don't forget to say the word, say the word, say the word. Don't forget to say the word, each and every time," she pointed to her mouth each time she sang, "Say the word." Marjorie gestured writing in the air when she sang, "Write a word, write a word, write a word." And then Marjorie mimed reading a book with her reading finger as she sang, "Read your book, read your book, read your book." Gestures, along with rhythm, beat, and repetition, are a sure way to imbed words and actions into long term memory. And just to check if this is working, just ask any student, "What do you do to make your writing easy to read?" Although they might not sing the actual song, they usually can tell you the key points because the chart has been "sung" repeatedly, bringing to life the steps involved (Figure 2.11).

Using Charts for Shared Reading

Once you start thinking about charts as shared sources of print in the classroom, in addition to their value as problem-solving tools, you will want to consider spending some time rereading charts as a shared reading experience, one in which the children have been cowriters and readers with the teacher (Mooney 1995). There are multiple benefits to making time for this endeavor. First and foremost, shared reading of charts in the classroom provides multiple opportunities for reminding children of the strategies they have been taught and are beginning to use. Whenever Kristine reads over her notes, for example, she is reminded of what she has heard and often thinks about how she is using what she has learned. Rereading useful strategies not only keeps key points in mind, it sets each listener up for reflection and to think, "What have I tried?" "What have I forgotten to try?" "What else might I try?"

Another added benefit of surrounding children with print is using shared reading, a technique originally developed by Don Holdaway (1979), in which the teacher reads a text, usually enlarged so that it can be seen by all the students, first to the children, then with the children, and ultimately, after several readings, the children read it by themselves (Moustafa 1997; Parkes 2000). Traditionally, the texts used are stories that have words and pictures that support the words, so that children learn about visual print in a meaningful way. Using charts as shared reading texts also helps children learn about print in a context that is meaningful. Repeated readings increase familiarity and confidence, allowing for the words and icons to be memorized, making these words and icons recognizable in other contexts, as well.

The shared reading of charts can be done anytime, but reading them just prior to teaching a lesson works as a sort of warm-up or welcoming signal that a new subject is being started. Doing this helps children transition from one topic to another and gets their heads around what they will be shifting into, whether reading, writing, or any other content area. It also creates a shared learning community. Ralph Peterson, in his book, *Life in a Crowded Place: Making a Learning Community* (1992), describes in depth each of the elements he believes necessary for creating a learning community: ceremony, ritual, rite, celebration, plan, and critique. Reading the charts together as one voice can become part of a classroom ceremony and ritual by setting a purpose and a tone to the experience ahead. In the last section, we introduced the children to a ritual for getting ready to read, with the hope that they would eventually develop their own rituals for getting started.

Many jokes abound about memory. "I wouldn't remember my lunch if it upped and bit me on the nose." "I wrote my to-do list, but then I forgot where I put it." But one thing that we have learned from brain research is that we can actually improve long-term memory simply by reviewing material over time and reflecting on that learning. Reactivating memory through repetition, reflection, and talk can happen once a week, once a semester, or even once a year, once something has been learned. John Medina suggests "Review Holidays," a day to review what has been learned so far, to help consolidate memory across all the grades as children progress through school (2008). Educators often refer to this as a "spiral curriculum." Repetition, rhythm, and rhyme can make this recursive rehearsal both fun and memorable.

Using Charts to Make Reading-Writing Connections

Repetition of a chant or a rhyme, rereading old charts, and revisiting taught concepts ensure the movement of information from short-term to long-term memory. There is yet one more way to move new information into known information, and that is making connections across curriculum. Though reading is a process of decoding and writing is a process of encoding, many of the skills and strategies we teach cross over between the two. Pointing out similarities, rather than differences, can reinforce children's understanding of process. For example, the retelling we do after we finish a story is a similar process to the oral telling we do when rehearsing our writing before committing it to the page. When we add more into an illustration in our writing, we envision a scene, and this is the same skill when we sketch a picture we are getting in our mind after reading a portion of a book.

Readers and writers also use analogous sources of information (Mermelstein 2006) when they make sure their reading and writing makes sense, sounds right, and looks right. Cross-checking is a valuable strategy whether reading a book, reading your own writing, or solving a math problem. Using the same prompts, the same language, across subject areas also increases the chance that children will transfer what they have learned in one area to other arenas. Leah Mermelstein articulates this beautifully in her book *Reading/Writing Connections in the K–2 Classroom* (2006) and gives many examples of this in action.

Because reading and writing go hand in hand, our charts and our teaching for writing could be just as closely linked. A popular method for helping children retell in reading is to teach them to "say the story across their fingers." Likewise, a popular method for helping children to plan their writing is to ask them to orally tell their story across their fingers. Imagine the power when these two ideas, which share the same language, have the same icon associated with them on the reading chart and the writing chart, and perhaps are even taught on the same day. When you make

connections between reading and writing, you cut your hunt for suitable visuals and language in half and children are exposed to it twice as much.

Using the same visuals and language on charts in related skills for reading and writing can help children make links between the two areas of literacy, making all your teaching more memorable and increasing the ability of children to access the information independently (Figure 2.12).

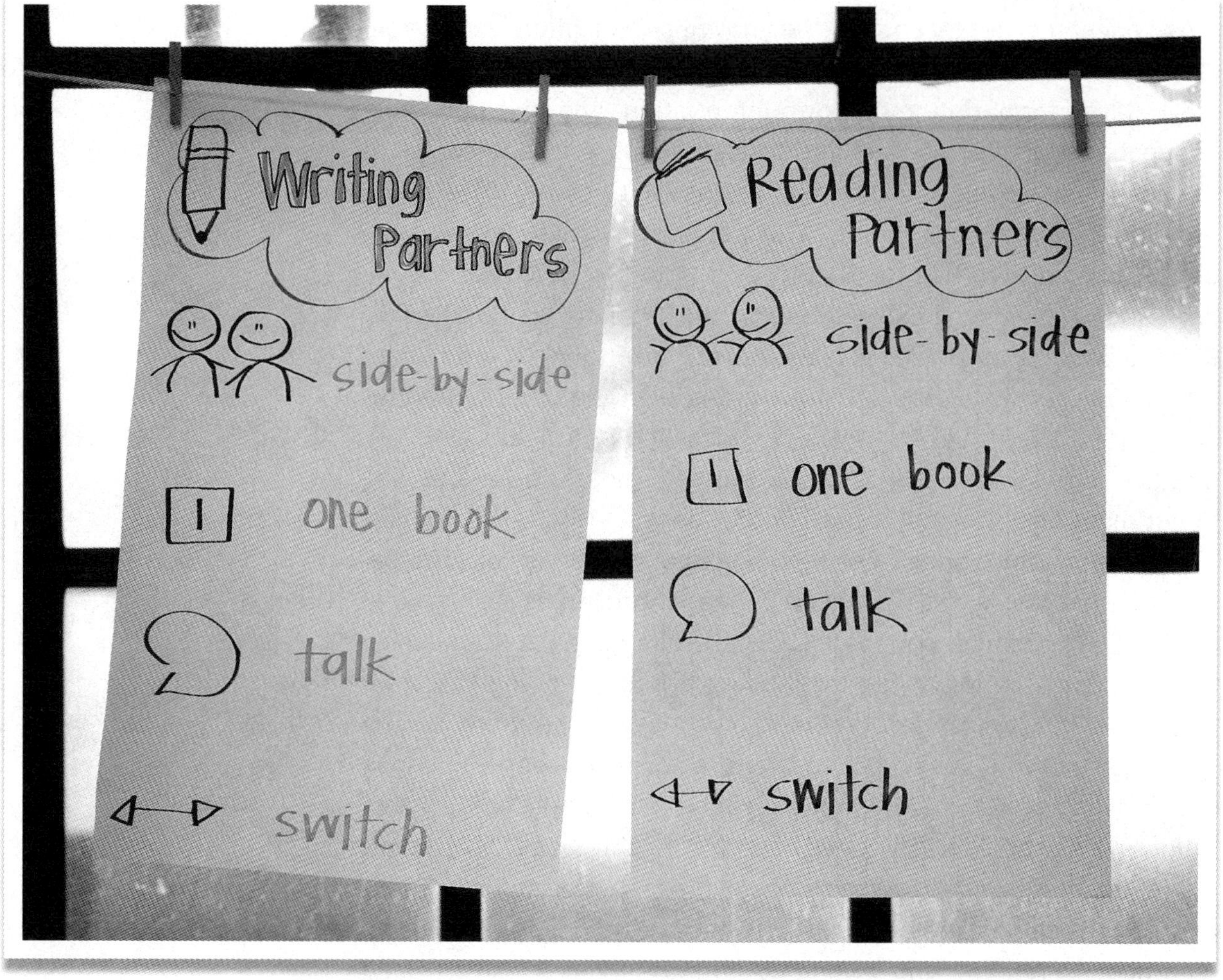

Figure 2.12 Similar symbols are used across many charts.

CHARTS IN ACTION: MAKING A CHART MEMORABLE FOR STUDENTS

We have learned how charts can reinforce our teaching and how to encourage the use of charts as helpful reminders of strategies being learned. In this lesson, Kristine tries to get a group of children to become more aware of what it takes to be a fluent reader. So far, they think that getting the words "right" means they are reading well. Over time, the classroom teacher has taught a variety of ways to read with fluency and the strategy chart that contains this list is hanging up next to other key reading charts in the classroom. In this case, a single chart is not going to provide an easy solution to the problem facing these students who seem to be struggling with fluency. This is definitely a case where repeated practice can help internalize the desired behavior, but how might the teacher use the chart to help encourage a more active resolve on the part of the students involved? After many discussions with colleagues and staff developers, Kristine decided to present to the students the dilemma she faced. She told them that she had taught the whole class a variety of ways readers could make their reading sound smooth that would also help bring everything they read to life by paying attention to the punctuation, the font, and the mood and tone of a book. But now, she wanted to know from them how they might come up with some ways for remembering the strategies, perhaps making their own chart that captured all this teaching in a way they would find most useful and that might help them become more fluent readers, so that no matter what they read it would come to life in their minds. The following transcript shows how this question evolved.

Lesson Focus: Readers Use Charts and Chants to Reflect and Make Goals Memorable

Materials:

- **Chart with strategies for reading fluently written on removable sticky notes**
- **Markers**
- **8½ × 11-inch copy paper**

"Okay, so I gathered you four together because I want us to work together on finding ways we can make our reading come to life, whether reading to ourselves or to others. As I have talked to each of you and listened to you read, I have noticed that most of you seem interested in figuring out the words and getting them right. Do you find this to be the case?"

Jacob, Triara, Kalib, and Jocelyn all nod their heads in agreement. Kristine immediately tells the children why she has gathered them together, but uses a conversational tone to talk about what she has noticed about their reading.

"I have also been talking to each of you about ways you can make your reading more enjoyable [Kristine points to the fluency chart hanging in the library area] *by scooping up more words at a time, making your voice sound like talking, paying attention to punctuation and font, and regulating the speed of your reading depending on what is happening in the story. But that's a lot to keep in mind as you read, right?"*

They nod again.

"So I was thinking that maybe you four could come up with some ways that would help you remember these strategies and maybe make your own chart that would help you read with fantastic fluency. What do you think?"

The children looked a bit skeptical.

"How would we do that?" Kalib asks.

"You already made a chart," Jocelyn adds.

"Hmm, that's true. Maybe we can take a closer look at the chart and think of some ways to make it fit you and what you might need to make it even better. Let's start by reading each point on the chart."

Together the group reads each bullet point on the chart. (See Figure 2.13.)

Figure 2.13 Talking about the strategies brings the chart back into the limelight.

- Use the chart to reinforce your words and to remind children that what they are going to work on today is not new. But even with the help of the chart, there is a lot to remember. Setting up a challenge to overcome can rile people up and get the juices flowing.

- Invite children to be a part of the solution to a problem, developing agency and encouraging them to be active participants in the lesson by having them reread the chart with a clear purpose.

"What things do you do the most? What things do you need reminding about?"

Kristine asks each child to take the strategy off the chart that they use the most. All four seem to notice the visual aspects of print, but not the meaning as much (Figure 2.14).

- Encourage children to reflect on what strategy on the chart they actually use and what strategy they hardly use, thus developing a more conscious awareness of what they are doing as readers.

Kristine brings the attention of the children to the bullet about regulating reading speed based on what is happening in the story.

"This one seems to be a bit trickier, huh?"

All four students nod.

"Perhaps we could make a rhyme or a chant that will help us to remember to try this one too?"

The children nod again. Kristine asks them to start thinking about a possible rhyme or chant while thinking a few words, aloud. *"Fast or slow, how could it go?"* After a bit of talk, and some coaching from Kristine, the students arrive at:

Fast or slow?

How should it go?

What happened here?

Say it clear!

Figure 2.14 One young student takes ownership of a strategy.

- Create a chant or cheer that summarizes the chart whenever you want to increase children's engagement and consciousness of a chart's purpose.

Thinking out loud helps the children get started. The teacher also realizes that this needs to be done quickly and without too much agonizing.

Kristine writes the words down on a piece of paper. Then, after a few rounds of chanting, she has the children choose a book to try out the strategy. As she notices moments where they forget, she softly whispers, *"Fast or slow?"* and the child finishes the chant, before rereading with a closer eye on matching the pace to what is happening in the story.

- Use the chant as a reminder of what the children need additional practice on.
- Encourage each child to use the chart to help themselves when they forget.

"So readers, remember that once we have figured out the words in our books, we also want to make our reading come to life and to make our reading more enjoyable by reading smoothly and fluently and not too slowly. And if you forget what you are working on, you can always try this little chant to help you remember. I'll make copies of the chant you created to put into your book baggies."

- Conclude the lesson by restating the purpose of the lesson and reminding students when they should use the chant.
- Remind students of the chart's purpose.
- Reflect on what strategies on the chart are actually used or hardly used.
- Involve students in finding ways to make the strategies memorable.

Next Steps:

The result of this session was not a new chart, but a way to remember one of the strategies the children were not using. Coming up with a clever chant is not the end goal, it is a vehicle for helping children get to the goal. It is also fun, which makes the children want to use it, which then gets them to practice the strategy more than they might otherwise. Reflection, response, and repetition has a huge impact on the effectiveness of any chart.

Last Words

As we move forward, keep in mind the importance of students using charts independently and the teacher's use of efficient time management when making charts, considering which parts to make ahead of time and which parts need to be made with the children. Always consider location, accessibility, and engagement. In addition, don't forget to use such time-tested techniques as repetition, rhyme, and song to make the charts memorable, making connections between reading and writing explicit and obvious.

In the next section, we will continue these ideas as we consider how to assess the success of our charts by looking at how charts are used, revised, and retired. In addition, we will give more classroom examples that will bring these many uses of charts to life. As you read forward, keep in mind what you have already put into place, what you want to put into place, and what you may want to change, add, or take away. Remember, less is often more, especially when it comes to young children.

If you leave this chapter with just one idea, though of course we know you have more, it would be that the goal of charts is that they help children work independently. The choices you make of where to hang them, when to make them, and how to use them in your teaching may be guided by your own time constraints and needs, but the question that should plague you most is: What will most help my students use them independently? From interactive writing to creating a tune, we want children to see the charts as theirs to use when they need them. The next section will help you judge the success of those efforts, and open up more possibilities to the

Location, accessibility, and engagement

Repetition, rhyme, and song

Making connections between reading and writing

Section 3

How Do I Assess the Success of My Charts?

Figure 3.1 Watching students at work can be one of the best assessments.

Last, but not least, let's think about how we can use our charts as co-teachers in the classroom, not only to teach, but to assess how our kids are doing. Have you ever wondered about the effectiveness of your charts? Have you ever considered having kids use the charts to help them self-assess their own work? Have you ever wondered when to take a chart down? In this section we give you tons of tips, recommendations, and checklists for using your charts to provide feedback on your teaching. We share questions that help children reflect and assess their own use of charts in order to develop goals. Then we show a series of focus lessons about ways they can use charts to reach these goals.

In addition, we discuss when to revise a chart and when to retire a chart. Just like each season we sort and clean out our closets, we need to do the same with our charts. It's not easy saying goodbye, whether to that favorite pair of now snug pants, or to that chart we so lovingly illustrated, but it is a necessary part of life. We will show you ways to do this that will make the effort very worthwhile.

There is a teaching maxim you might have heard that goes something like, "If they haven't learned it, you haven't taught it." Just think back to a lesson you thought was rock star dynamic, but which had little or no impact on student work. While humbling for sure, it is most important to realize that what students do (or don't do) as a result of our teaching gives us the best feedback. This is one of the best forms of assessment. In this section, we will tackle that very idea: assessment. We will look at both formal and informal assessments that we can use to measure the "stickiness" of both our teaching and the charts that support it (Figure 3.1). Additionally, we will look at assessing levels of student independence, as well as the products that students produce. Frequently in this book, we have explored the ways that we can use charts and tools to help students work actively and independently. In this section, we tackle the questions: Did it work? Have students learned what we have taught? And ultimately, how can we as teachers reflect on the usefulness of our charts and make decisions about when to revise or retire a chart?

We will start with:

● helping children reflect on their own learning and create some goals

● encouraging children's independent and active use of charts when needed

● using questioning to help children take on a reflective stance

● stepping back and observing our own teaching.

Then we will spy on some children as they use charts to help notice the types of crafting strategies they tend to use, or not use, when they revise their writing.

How Did I Do? Children Can and Should Self-Assess

One of the goals we have as teachers is that our students leave us as citizens that will make the world a better place. One of the traits we work to instill is an active stance toward their own learning. Students should decide what they need to work on, be allowed to make mistakes, and then reflect on how they have achieved their goals. Charts provide a concrete tool with which children can practice this life skill.

Following are some easy, but powerful, tips to help children reflect and assess.

- Touch and tell: Partners can go to charts and take turns touching the different teaching on the chart and tell their partner how or where they used it. They can then choose something they didn't try and go back and try it.

- Chart share: Teachers can end a workshop with the question: What chart did you use today and how did it help you? Students can share in small groups or in a circle.

- Small copies of big charts: Children can have small copies of big charts and use them as checklists (Figure 3.2). In writing they might tally how many times they tried a certain skill, and then make a goal to try something that doesn't have as many tally marks. In reading they might reflect on the strategies they used, or think about what else they could try.

Figure 3.2 The teacher, Ms. Newman, has prepared small versions of an exemplar chart for children to have close by.

- Expert sticky note: When you see a child has applied a skill or a strategy from a chart, they can put their name on a sticky note and hang it next to that item (Figure 3.3). Then if another student needs help with that strategy, they can "ask the experts."

- Set a goal: Before children go off to read or write, they can mark the chart they plan to use with a sticky note that has their name on it. At partner time, they can reflect on where or how they used that chart.

When these activities happen frequently, they cease to be novelties and start to become everyday practice for children. Often what begins intentionally, when repeated, slips into habit, so that children habitually look back over charts and their own work to compare and set goals. One first-grade teacher shared a story with us about such a situation. She had been working hard to direct children to use charts when they felt stuck or "done." In writing workshop one day, a boy turned to ask his partner a question, to which the partner promptly replied, "Don't ask me, ask the chart!"

Thinking Through Questioning: The Greatest Gift a Teacher Can Give

In the book *Already Ready* (2008) by Katie Wood Ray and Matt Glover, they sagely advise that we should be asking children questions, even if they don't have the answers yet, because this will teach students that these are the types of things that writers and readers think about. If questions serve as prompts for thinking, then whenever we work with children we want to be asking questions around the ways they are using charts. For example, "I notice you seem a bit stuck. Is there a chart in the room that might help you?" Even if they haven't used them yet, the questioning implies that they should. Just think of the mom-ism, "Are you really going to wear that?" as the model of a question that

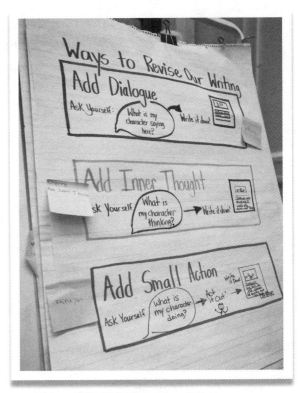

Figure 3.3 Children can put their names next to the strategy they plan to work on as writers.

Figure 3.4 Moveable sticky notes allow the goals (from the chart in Figure 3.3) to go from page to page and from book to book.

speaks volumes! The following are questions that have worked for teachers to help children reflect and assess on their use of charts (see Appendix D):

- What charts have you used today? How have they helped you?

- Can you show me a place where the charts helped you?

- What are you working on? Is there a chart that can help you do that?

- Which chart do you use the most? Why?

- Which chart don't you use? Why?

- What goals have you set for yourself? Which chart will help you?

- If you could make a chart, what would you make?

In the beginning, you may be met with blank stares, or a fumbled answer. In one case, when asked if she had used a chart, a child responded, "But that has all the answers on it!" Talking with children about charts in this way sets a precedent for how charts should be used in the classroom and also allows you to work through any hidden misconceptions as to their purpose (Figure 3.5). One way to scaffold this work with students is to teach lessons about ways to use charts in these ways.

A series of focus lessons around this topic might include:

- Readers/writers reread the charts before they start working. This helps us remember all the things we know about reading/writing.

- When we get a little tired of working, we can give our brains a little rest and read the charts. This helps us remember what we need to be thinking about when we go back to our work.

- When readers/writers get stuck, we can go to the charts to help us. We might reread each part of the chart until we find the tip that will help us get unstuck.

- When readers/writers are done, we bring our work to the chart and check: did I do each of these things?

Figure 3.5 Talking about charts with a student.

Looking and Listening for Signs of Our Own Teaching

Assessment is not a test, it is a way to get feedback on our teaching. In *The Hundred Languages of Children*, Loris Malaguzzi (1998) advised teachers to "stand aside for a while and leave room for learning, observe carefully what children do, and then, if you have understood well, perhaps teaching will be different from before" (82). We are often so busy teaching that we don't have time to step back and just watch, but when we do, a whole private world opens up to us. When you see Sammy slowly building his books into a tower of biblical proportions, you have one possible answer to the burning question: Why isn't Sammy moving as a reader? Taking time to observe how children are using charts will help you assess the success of your charting and teaching, providing some possible answers to the question, "Are the charts being actively used by children?" For one workshop, or part of a workshop, you might make a grid (see following table and Appendix E).

Names	Looks at Chart	Walks to Chart	Uses Individual Charts	Notes
1.				
2.				

Keeping track of behaviors helps teachers know how charts are being used.

Record with tallies who is using what chart. Then you might teach a few lessons or work with a few small groups to engage children more with the charts, especially when working independently.

In addition to assessing who is using the charts, we want to use charts to study the work our students are doing. If you have taught children to self-assess and put their name on a sticky note next to the strategy they are using, you have a clear visual cue of which teaching points are "sticking." You might then decide to reteach a specific skill or strategy. If you sometimes feel like you can't name exactly what your student's writing needs, it can be helpful to take a stack of stories and look at a specific chart. Which children are using what you have taught, and who are not? Looking at student writing, or student sticky notes, against the charts you have made gives you a tangible and quick assessment of what children have learned, not just what you have taught.

The same goes for reading. Oftentimes we will hear teachers say, "Retelling is so hard for my class!" If this sounds like you, freeze for a moment and look to the chart you have for student retelling. What does it say? If it is a chart of a hand with the words *first*, *then*, *next*, *after that*, and *finally*, your children may use those ordinal words when retelling and still miss the big points of the story. However, if your chart about retelling says, "Use character names, say what the character did or where the character went in the first few pages, name any big feelings," and so on, you can better assess not only that children are using what was taught, but whether or not they understand what was taught. Some children also need these more specific details to help them at first. You might keep a small copy of that chart with you when you listen to students read and retell so you can listen for how they use the elements you have taught.

Sharing Charts and Chart Assessments with Evaluators

Teacher evaluation has become a hot topic in schools lately. Fortunately, all this work you are doing with charts can become a tool for you to share the incredible teaching and learning that is happening in your classroom with any evaluator. You might tour your classroom with an administrator or an evaluator to showcase the pathway your

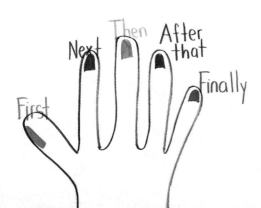

teaching has taken with your students. Because charts capture the most important work that you are teaching, it can be made clear in a snapshot to an administrator or an evaluator that you have set rigorous goals (as indicated by the headings) and taught students a variety of ways to reach those goals (as indicated by the words and visuals that comprise the rest of the chart).

Perhaps even more importantly, sharing your assessments of student work against the charts, or your assessments of the ways students use the charts, illustrates the way you use assessment to inform instruction. You might take evidence of this in the form of a checklist or student work to your evaluator and share how it has informed and changed your teaching. Kristine once brought a pile of student work and small copies of her charts to a postobservation meeting. She was able to share with her evaluator that she had assessed her student writing against these charts and had found that many of the students had met her goals for focus, but elaboration was still proving to be tricky. She then explained her next steps in teaching elaboration and the ways she might use charts to help this skill "stick" more with her first-grade students.

Using your charts, and the assessments you do with them, provides clear examples to evaluators of the rigor of your instruction and the role assessment plays in your teaching. Your work with charts and related assessments is a powerful tool for communicating the daily work of your classroom to those who may only see it from time to time.

Assessing Our Charts: Just What Should We Look For?

Many states are moving toward teacher evaluation systems based not only on observation, but on questioning designed to get behind each teacher's thought processes, and then the teacher is asked to reflect on the decisions she or he made and think about how effective each decision was in helping children learn. As we mentioned in the Introduction ("Charting Our Course" section), charts are often used as an indicator of the quality of instruction happening in a classroom and many administrative checklists include charts among the categories to be evaluated. So just what should we be looking for when we walk into a classroom (even our own) and look at the charts? How do we find out why they are hanging up in the room and how they are being used? What questions might we ask to find out some possible answers? What qualities should we be looking for in a chart? Although this last question is what this entire book is about, we have some specific suggestions for both teacher and evaluator alike.

When you walk into a classroom, one thing to look for is the *type* of charts hanging around the room. For this you can use the "Field Guide to Types of Charts" found in Appendix A and in color on the inside front cover. This chart names and defines the types of charts typically found in classrooms. Once you have named the variety of charts, you can begin taking a closer look at the quantity and quality of the charts. The following list includes some key elements of successful charts to look for as you assess:

- The charts are clear, easy to understand, and easy to find.
- The content on each chart is current and supports increasing complex skills.
- The purpose for the chart is clear.
- The chart includes the steps for how to do specific strategies or procedures.
- The chart has visuals, including symbols, pictures, and/or photographs that support and illustrate the words.
- Exemplars, such as student examples and mentor texts, are added to the chart and annotated.
- Some charts are made portable or customized and can be seen actively in use by the children.

Another way to learn about the charts is to ask the children. The "Self-Assessment Sheet" in Appendix D can give you some ideas for the kinds of questions you might ask children about the charts surrounding them. You can ask, "Which chart do you find the most helpful or use the most? Which charts do you no longer need to help you?" Children can be encouraged to discuss a chart and to give reasons for what is on it and why. Do the children use any of the charts to reflect and self-assess their own work, creating goals for themselves? To help you observe and record children's use of charts and other tools in the classroom, you can use the "Chart Behaviors Observation Sheet" (Appendix E). You can tell a lot about expectations, both behavioral and educational, when you talk to children about the charts in their room. Charts should set clear expectations and they often indicate what is valued in the classroom. This is something we all can learn from.

CHARTS IN ACTION: USING CHARTS TO SELF-ASSESS

Revision can be a tricky time for students. They often add a word or two and then cap their pens with a satisfied sigh. Our job as teachers is to engage writers in deeper, more thoughtful revision, which can be exceedingly difficult for five-, six-, and seven-year-olds, because rereading does not seem as fun as starting anew. Finding ways to help children realize that revision is actually fun requires us to teach children that they are not only making something new, but making something better. Creating small copies of large charts and using those as a springboard for reflection and revision can add a more dynamic element to this challenging part of the writing process.

Lesson Focus: To teach children how to use small versions of a class craft chart to self-assess the kinds of revision strategies being used and to help in making goals and plans for further revision.

Materials:

- **Photograph of the class craft chart reproduced on 8½ × 11-inch paper, one for the teacher, and one for each member of the group**

- **Felt-tip pens, one for each member of the group**

- **The writing students have been working on, along with their writing folders**

"Okay, everyone, I have kind of a special treat for you today! I thought since we have been working so hard on making our writing 'real nail-biters,' we might be able to use our chart to see how we did! First I want to show you how I am going to use this tool, ready?"

Ms. Levy holds up the chart and a piece of her own writing and uncaps her felt-tip pen.

"Every time I find one of the things on the chart in my writing, I am going to make a tally on the chart. Okay, here I go!"

Ms. Levy finds dialogue and makes a tally next to the part of the chart that reads *talking*. Going on, she makes a few more tallies next to *talking* and a few next to *actions*. The students begin chiming in, **"Look—talking!"** When she finishes two pages she stops.

- Show children exactly how you want them to use the strategy chart.

- Use tally marks rather than check marks to emphasize that you want the children to use each strategy lots of times. The check implies "did it and done."

"Do you see how I was doing that? I was going page by page and every time I saw something from the chart that I did in my writing, I made a tally! I also noticed something, too. Give me a thumbs-up if you saw it. I don't have any feelings! Yeesh. Look, I have five tallies next to dialogue and six next to actions and none next to feelings! I need to go back and add some in! Okay, your turn!"

■ Use writing that has some obvious gaps to make it easy for children to notice which strategies have not been used as much as others (Figure 3.6).

Ms. Levy passes out the rest of the small charts to the students in the group, and they begin to read their writing and tally what they find they have done on the individual charts.

Aliyah says, **"Hey! I only put talking in my pictures!"** Ms. Levy leans in and whispers, *"So what are you thinking?"* Aliyah responds, **"I better put some in my words!"** and gets to work diligently writing some of the dialogue from her pictures into her words.

Ms. Levy bounces from student to student coaching them. She whispers to John, *"Don't forget to tally!"* The whispering is a way to quietly remind children what they can do or try. As they get through their first piece, Ms. Levy stops them.

Figure 3.6 Ms. Levy sets the children up to use the chart again and again.

■ Create one or two charts that become touchstones for the unit and return to them often, so the children know them well.

"Okay, whoa, that was so . . . much . . . fun! And Aliyah noticed something super interesting. She noticed she only had talking in her pictures! Can you look at your minichart right now and see what you did an amazing job on? What part has the most tallies?"

John yells, **"Actions!"** and Jordan has a few tallies next to each one, and says, **"I did them all!"**

■ Tallies help children reflect more easily than looking again at their writing because there is a clear quantity, and it is obvious that they have done some things more than others.

"Okay, so look hard now, which one or two things do you need to go back and do more of? Look for a spot on your minichart where you don't have many tallies."

John quickly puts his fingers on **talking** and **feeling**, Aliyah continues to have her finger on **talking**, Jordan looks a little confused and says, "I did them all!" Ms. Levy quickly directs the students to start finding spots where they can add those great things and leans into Jordan, who she sees only has two to three tallies by each thing.

"Jordan, sometimes the job we give ourselves is really big, like maybe we don't try to do something once, we try to do it like, maybe, like five times, or even ten times!"

Jordan's eyes get big, **"Ten times?"** Ms. Levy nods sagely and Jordan looks back at his sheet. **"I can add talking ten times, no fifteen times, no twenty!"** he says. Ms. Levy smiles and nods and Jordan starts writing. The teacher lets Jordan dream big. This may make his writing a little chaotic, but he will have lots of practice writing dialogue!

■ Make small versions of some of your class charts and get children to physically interact with them.

■ When children mark up a chart, they actually create a plan for revision that is customized to their writing needs.

Ms. Levy coaches each child, giving tips as he or she writes. After another minute or so, she stops the group.

CHARTS IN ACTION

"Okay, smart work everyone, I know you aren't done so I will be quick. You all did something really smart here today—you looked at your writing and at the minichart and you thought two things. First you learned what you do a lot of, what you are really good at! Then you thought what you could do more and you set a goal. Writers, whenever you look at charts, you can use them like this: to think about what you do really well, and to set a goal for something else to try!"

■ Goal setting is easy because of the concrete nature of the activity.

■ Extend the learning so that children might do this type of reflection whether they have small copies of the big charts or not.

Next Steps:

This might become a monthly routine in Ms. Levy's class to help children assess what they have tried and set goals for what to revise in their writing. It takes away the checklist "did it" or "need it" type of black-and-whiteness. It looks at number of times a child has tried something and therefore leads to a closer look at the process the child is using. Children can also keep this small chart in a sheet protector and tally with a dry erase marker so they can redo the process on a new piece. This can also be done on the large class chart by having children write their names on sticky notes and the number of times they have tried something, then placing their sticky notes next to each craft move they have tried. (See Figure 3.7.) This works well when you want a quick whole-class assessment of what qualities of good writing children are using the most and the least.

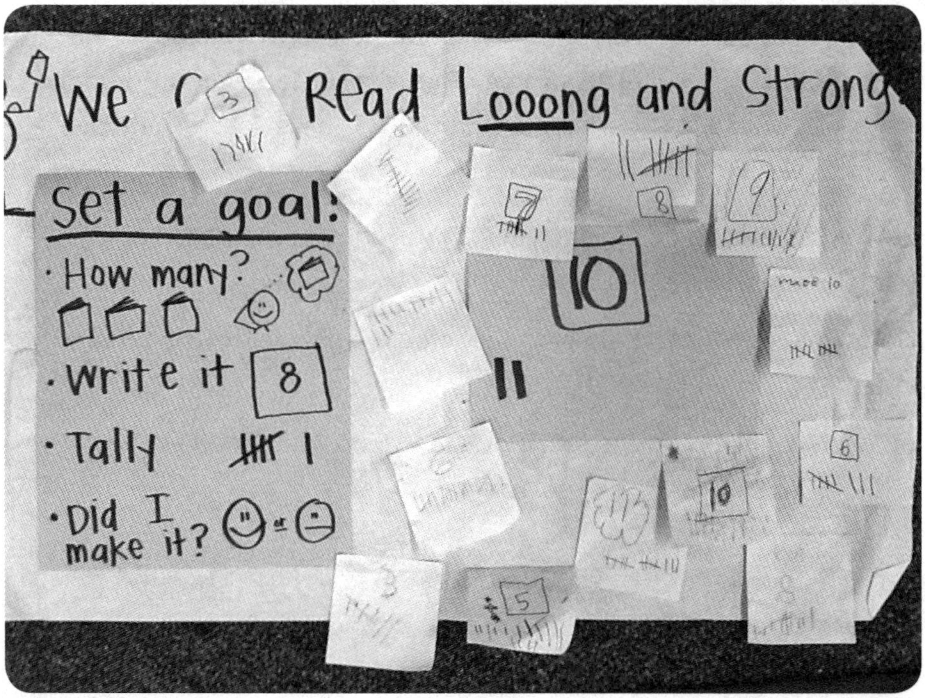

Figure 3.7 Children add sticky notes to a chart to share the day's reading work.

Revise or Retire Charts When the Time Is Right

As you may recall from the Introduction, the Reggio Emilia schools in Italy consider the environment the third teacher in a school, but in order to act as the teacher for the child, this environment must also be flexible and able to undergo frequent modifications by the children and teachers to remain current and responsive to their needs (Gandini 1998). This is a collaborative process done with the children and teachers both. If our charts are to act as teachers, they, too, must be flexible and kept up-to-date, which leads to the question, "When do I revise a chart or decide to retire it?" We will provide some suggestions and insights that have worked for us in our own classrooms and in classrooms across the world.

Revising: What Is Old Becomes New Again

One way to keep charts alive and actively used in the classroom is to revise them, to change them in some way. When something becomes too familiar, it is like it becomes invisible, we simply stop seeing it. That is, unless it goes missing or it is moved to a new location. Anyone who has ever rearranged a living room or replaced one photo on the wall with a more current photo has experienced this effect. What is old becomes new again. Tim Rasinski in his book *The Fluent Reader* (2010) talks about the power of multiple readings of shared reading texts, but acknowledges that after a while the children simply do a rote telling of the text based on memory and no longer look at the words. To counteract this effect, he suggests innovating on the text, or if it is a poem or song, adding some new verses. Changing the words forces children to attend to the print on the page again. This has the added benefit of making the familiar new again, which lifts the level of engagement and interest. The same goes for charts.

When we think about revision, the typical things that come to mind are adding, taking away, or moving around. The goal of revision is to enhance the clarity and the richness of a text to engage the anticipated readers. It is also considered the favorite part of the writing process by many professional writers. In fact many authors, such as Georgia Heard, Barry Lane, and Lucy Calkins, have written whole books on the topic of revision. Lucy Calkins always says that revision is a compliment to the writer's best writing. With this in mind, there are several ways teachers can revise the charts hanging in their classrooms.

- Add to the chart, either a new strategy, a new example, or a new picture.
- Take away something that is no longer needed because it has been learned by all.
- Move the chart to a new location, either physically or by reducing it and placing it in children's hands.

Teachers often add strategies to charts as they teach a new strategy, either during a lesson or later during a share time when students are gathered together to reflect and consider what worked or made the work easier. There is nothing that draws children's attention quicker than when the teacher picks up a marker and begins to write something new in front of them. They also attend with equal focus when the teacher physically adds a sentence strip or sheet of paper with the new strategy written and illustrated on it to emphasize the teaching point. Adding to a chart also provides an opportunity to celebrate all that the children are learning and lets them know they have many ways to make something better or to deal with any difficulty that might arise.

Taking away something that is no longer needed is always a reason to celebrate. This signals progress, an outgrowing, and gives everyone a sense of accomplishment, a job well done. Whenever a strategy is removed from a chart, it should be done ceremoniously and with some reflection about why it is being removed and what it says about us as learners and students. For example, in one first-grade classroom, the children had outgrown the strategy of looking at the picture and the first letter to predict what the word might be on the page. The teacher pointed out that everyone was using this strategy without ever needing to look at the chart. In addition, it was no longer the most useful strategy for figuring out words in the books they were now reading. They had more efficient, more "grown-up" strategies to use now.

"I have been looking at our 'Figuring Out Tricky Words' chart and I was noticing that there are some strategies we all know, and in fact, are not that useful anymore. That makes me think that we can take down the ones we don't need or use anymore. Let's look over the chart and think about which things we do all the time without even thinking, and which things we sometimes need a reminder to help us. Turn and tell your partner what strategies you

do all the time and which ones you sometimes need a reminder." Actively involving the children in this decision-making process ensures their empowerment and feelings of accomplishment. To further emphasize the huge growth taking place, you may want to suggest that this discarded strategy might actually be very helpful to the grade below. Just like we hand down outgrown clothing to younger siblings, we can hand down outgrown strategies to younger students in the school. How amazing to ask a group of students to make a special delivery of one of their no longer needed strategy charts to a class that might now need those very same strategies.

Sometimes simply moving a chart can make it feel new again. There is no question that a chart that has been hanging in the same spot for over a month is part of the wallpaper and no longer noticed. In fact, it has probably started to turn a bit yellow at the edges, with portions drooping and falling off, not to mention growing rather dusty. If you see any charts in this condition, it is a sure sign they need some attention and updating. The easiest and quickest solution is to move the chart to a new location, announcing this move with great fanfare. "Writers, we are going to be doing a lot of revision work getting our writing ready to publish, so I am going to put all our charts about revision and craft together over here next to our writing center where our revision tools are located. If you are looking for some revision tips, now you know where exactly to look!"

You can also bring these charts back to life by creating small versions that can be placed directly into children's hands, on tables, or into folders or notebooks. The advantage of making smaller, more accessible versions of charts is that it reinforces not only what you have taught, but how to use the resources to actively help you as needed. Some charts can easily be made into checklists where children can tally how many times they use a specific strategy and create goals for what to work on next.

Although the whole-class charts you create often emphasize the teaching of the current unit of study, there are many other charts, from previous units of study in particular, that remain pertinent and important to any unit. Unfortunately, this is not always obvious to our children unless we make it obvious. Constant, explicit teaching into how to use these charts as productive tools that will make our reading and writing work easier is a necessary part of our teaching. Handing over a chart to a child can be like a gift in that it makes life easier in some small way. It is no longer for everyone, it has been customized for you. *You.* "You can take this and use it to make your reading/writing extraordinary in ways that will surprise you even more than me."

Retiring: When to Retire a Chart

To retire has many meanings and many implications. Some of the words attached to the word *retire* are *quit, resign, leave, withdraw, pull out, vacate, exit,* and *recede.* These words alone might seem somewhat empty, lonely, or sad. Retirement, on the other hand, can often be seen as a lifelong goal to strive toward, something to celebrate. Whether the experience is positive or negative depends on choice and action. The same goes for the charts we have hanging up in the classroom.

Charts are made by teachers to make their teaching visible, understandable, and doable. Therefore, every chart is critical and important in helping students feel they have resources available to help them be successful in the tasks at hand. Teachers reinforce these ideas every time they refer to a chart while conferring, when teaching a minilesson, and when teaching a small group. But when do we teach our children they have outgrown some charts or some strategies on the chart? When should some charts begin to recede or just plain leave? The first thing to think about is the purpose for the chart and whether or not it is still fulfilling this purpose. Be aware of next steps. Look at what is on your current charts and then think, "What if all my students are doing all of these things?" "What are they not yet doing?" These can lead to a shared class discussion about what you see and what you wonder, using the class charts as a touchstone to base your discussion upon.

Once the class has discussed which charts are most useful, which charts are needed occasionally, and which charts are no longer needed, then the class can make some decisions about which charts to put away or give away. The first charts to be retired are often those created at the beginning of the year that deal with routines and procedures, like how to come to the rug for a minilesson or how to sit with a partner. Teachers often love these charts the most, especially if they have endearing photographs of their children taken during those early days of the school year. If some charts have sentimental value, they can be hard to get rid of even if no longer necessary. But remember what was discussed earlier about prime real estate and available wall space. It is valuable, but limited. One suggestion is to scrapbook the charts by putting these oldies but goodies together into a big book by making a cover and adding it to the big book collection in your library where you can invite children to read whenever they want to remember how they used to look and be at the beginning of the year.

Another reason to retire a chart is when it is specific to a genre or unit of study that is no longer a focus in the classroom. A favorite study may have been the folktale unit, but charts specific to the genre, like the ones describing the characteristics of a folktale or that compare and contrast several folktales, may not be that useful once the children are no longer reading and writing folktales. Look around your classroom for any charts that were created during earlier units of study and ask whether the content on the chart is still pertinent to what your children are currently studying. An example of this might be a chart about choosing books. If book shopping is down pat in your classroom, it's time to say "bon voyage!" to that chart. These types of charts can be withdrawn from public view. You might want to photograph the chart first so you have it as a reminder of what you taught in the unit. You could also hang the charts in your closet on skirt hangers and have a raffle at the end of the year, sending each child home with one of the retired class charts.

CHARTS IN ACTION: BRINGING A CHART BACK TO LIFE BY REVISING

When we get ready to start studying a new subject or a new genre, we often think about all that is different and all that is new to be learned, and new can sometimes be scary. We have found that instead of starting with all that is different, we start with all that is the same, as this propels children forward and upward more quickly because they are boosted up by what they already know. On this day, the goal was for the children in this collaborative team teaching classroom not to be intimidated by the new genre, but to feel powerful and strong as they began this new unit of study on information writing.

When it comes to writing, the one thing that rarely changes is the process, so Mr. Weaver and Marjorie decided to start by bringing back the charts on writing process and generating topics that the class had created during the first narrative units of study. One chart was about the writing process represented in a never-ending circle and the other was a strategy chart showing three ways writers might use to come up with stories. The process chart did not need to be revised, but the chart on generating stories needed to be tweaked so it would work for helping children find lots of topics for nonnarrative writing.

Lesson Focus: To reinforce the writing process and to help children learn, they can generate topics for information books by revisiting strategies learned during a previous narrative genre study.

Materials:

- Writing process chart (made during an earlier unit of study)
- Generating story ideas chart (made during an earlier unit of study)
- Four large sticky notes with chart revisions written out ahead of time inside of speech bubbles
- Small sticky notes in the same (or similar) three colors used on the generating story ideas chart

"Published authors. Yes, you! As we look around we see authors who have published several books. And as published authors, you know a lot about how to write a book: getting ideas, planning, getting those ideas down on paper, revising to make the story even better, and editing to make your books easy to read for every single reader. This is what we call the writing process."

- Give children labels they have earned through hard work and effort as it celebrates agency, not ability.

Marjorie and Mr. Weaver point to the writing process chart, which has been brought back out for this lesson.

■ Reference charts in the classroom that have been created during previous units of study because it reminds children of what they already know and points out that they can use this knowledge anytime, regardless of the unit of study.

■ Pull out charts previously made together with the class to set children up to work independently. This sends the message, "You have done this before."

"And today we are going to teach you how the writing process is the same no matter what kind of writing you do. We are going to begin writing information books that teach people all about things we know really well. And the first part of the writing process is to come up with topics to write about. Well, guess what? You can find ideas for topics you are experts on in the very same places you looked to find story topics: places, people, and things."

Marjorie gestures toward the chart on generating ideas that they created during an earlier unit on personal narrative writing.

"Remember when we found stories hiding in the places, people, and things that are a part of our lives? Well, guess what? We can look in the very same places to find topics we know a lot about. It will just take a bit of revising. Watch how we can revise our chart on generating stories so that it will help us come up with topics for the information books we will be writing next.

"First I am going to read the heading. Looking for a story! Hmm. Story. We are not going to be writing stories, we are going to be writing information books that teach about a topic. So, I can just change the word story to the word topic."

■ Let children in on the fact that charts can be revised. It also gets the children to look at the chart with fresh eyes.

Mr. Weaver sticks the new label over the word story in the heading. Then Marjorie rereads the revised heading.

"Now the heading reads, 'Looking for a topic?' Okay, now let's look at the suggestions for where to find ideas for stories. The first suggestion is places. Hmm. Could places help us come up with ideas for what we might be expert enough to teach others and turn into a book?"

Figure 3.8 Simply changing one word can make a chart more universal.

- Paste a new word or phrase over the old word or phrase, immediately updating the chart. This is just one way to revise (Figure 3.8).

- Add a new graphic or picture to the chart to make it current.

Marjorie tilts her head slightly to the side, finger on chin, contemplating the question, showing the internal tug of war and letting children know that these decisions are not made lightly.

"Yes, if we go to some places each and every day, then of course we are experts on those places. Let's add that tip to places."

Marjorie removes a talk bubble from her clipboard on which she has prewritten "each and every day" and hands it to Mr. Weaver, who adds it next to the first bullet on the chart.

- Prewrite the revisions when you plan to do more than one or two so you can quickly highlight each addition to the chart.

- Always have chart materials ready and easily accessible.

- Use symbols the children will understand like the speech bubble, which makes the chart "talk."

"The next suggestion is to remember times spent with special people in our lives. Hmm. Is it possible that we could be experts on people we know? I guess so, especially if we know these people really, really well. Let's add that tip next to people."

The talk bubble with the words **really, really well** is placed next to the second bullet on the chart by Mr. Weaver. Once again, the teacher shows how she looks to a strategy and imagines how it might work when writing a different genre. Emphasizing what is the same can be even more powerful than noting how things are different. Simply adding the one line, like **each and every day** or **really, really well**, points out the importance of experience to become an expert.

"Now, the last suggestion on this chart is to think about things we do. Could this lead to ideas about things we are experts on? Hmm. Yes, if we do something all the time, then we are probably experts and could teach others to do the same thing. We can add that tip to the chart."

Mr. Weaver adds the talk bubble with the words **all the time** written on it to the chart.

- The decision to use short, catchy phrases was deliberate. Think of the point of purchase signs used in the grocery store and their purpose—to grab your attention and make you want to buy.

- Notice the arrows and how they reinforce the idea of having a repertoire: If one strategy doesn't work, try another, and another.

"Now, let's read our newly revised chart all together:

Looking for a topic? Try thinking about . . .

Places you go *each and every day!*

People you know *really, really well!*

Things you do *all the time!*

- The shared reading makes the chart more memorable, plus it helps ensure that all the children will be able to read the chart.

"So, writers, let's try to use our newly revised chart to help us come up with ideas for topics we could teach and write lots of books about. On each table there are three different-colored sticky notes to jot your topics on. The yellow sticky note is for the ideas you get by thinking about places you go."

Figure 3.9 The small sticky notes remind children of the tools they have been given and the color-coding helps remember which strategy the tools go with.

Marjorie puts a sample yellow sticky note next to the big yellow sticky note on the chart that says **Places you go**. (See Figure 3.9.)

- Use color-coding.
- Plan for ways children can interact with the chart.

"We didn't have orange sticky notes to match this big orange note on the chart for **People** *you know, so we will use these pink sticky notes for the ideas you get by thinking about people you know really, really well."*

The pink sticky note is put next to the big orange note on the chart.

"And last but not least, the green sticky note is for things you do all the time."

This last sticky note is put up on the chart.

"We can't wait to hear about all the ideas you have for topics to write about. Let's get started!"

The children scurried off to gather their special sticky notes and get started. (See Figure 3.10.)

Next Steps:

As the children jot down their ideas on the sticky notes, you can confer into the topics students loved to write about during the narrative unit and teach how that can become an information book topic. "The Time I Got My First Video Game" can become "All About Video Games!" "The Day My Baby Brother Was Born" might become "All About Babies." If some children have trouble thinking of topics even with these prompts, you might have them make a small chart titled, "What I Do Each and Every Day." They could add one box for what they do each morning, a box for what they do every day in school, another for each afternoon, and one more for each evening. For people, they could create a box for each person they know really well and begin to sketch and jot all they know about each of them. They could create a little booklet they carry around with them and jot down the things they do all the time. On this particular day, when the children came back together for the whole-class share, they added all their sticky notes to the chart. When they saw the chart filled with ideas for topics, they were ecstatic. The workshop ended with a hearty round of applause.

Throughout the unit, children can add (and subtract) sticky notes to the chart as they generate and use ideas. This chart will become a handy tool throughout the unit as the children need ideas to write more information books.

Figure 3.10 The teacher, Mr. Weaver, coaches into topic choice.

CHARTS IN ACTION

Last Words

Charts help to make our teaching explicit and clear by providing step-by-step directions and key tips and strategies for how to do something. But knowing for sure whether these charts are clear to our students requires us to step back and observe explicit student behaviors. How do they actually use the charts? When do they use them and why? If you find a chart is not being used and it hangs limp and lifeless in a corner, all is not lost. Through lessons, small groups, and revision strips or sticky notes, it can be resurrected to support readers and writers once again. It is ultimately your belief in the strength and value of these tools that will drive their success.

These observations can lead to further questions and interviews where we dig a little deeper into how the charts are being used by our children. We can use charts to assess what our students understand by laying their work alongside the charts, which are a record of our teaching. And, most importantly, children can use charts as guideposts and goalposts to measure accomplishments and create goals worth striving toward. Finally, if the environment is the third teacher, we need to make sure that what is up on the walls and hanging from the ceiling is clear, interactive, and purposeful. That is how you assess the success of your charts.

Last, Last Words

When we began the journey of writing this book together, we puzzled over the title for quite a while. We struggled the same way we struggle over headings on charts: How do we capture so much in a few catchy words? What is it that we were really trying to say? Then it struck us: It wasn't just about making charts, it was about creating smarter charts. This is not a book that asks you to reinvent the wheel, but rather take a long hard look at the wheel and ask: Is it working? How can we make it better? How do we get to the root of what charts are supposed to do: help create independent readers and writers?

The answer is not one thing but many things that will help us reach this lofty goal. For some, it will be clearer visuals, more precise language, or even conquering the fear of drawing people. For others, it might be the idea of co-creating charts with students, using table tents in a room with no wall space, or keeping charts interactive with large bright sticky notes. For still others, it may be the idea that charts help children self-assess, or that charts help teachers self-assess, or even that charts should be revised and retired when the time is right. Whatever big ideas and helpful tips you have gathered from this book, we hope that you share them with colleagues and innovate on them in your own classroom. The smartest charts, of course, will be the ones you make with the intention of helping our smallest readers and writers conquer the big work of being independent problem solvers and active participants in their own learning.

Happy charting!

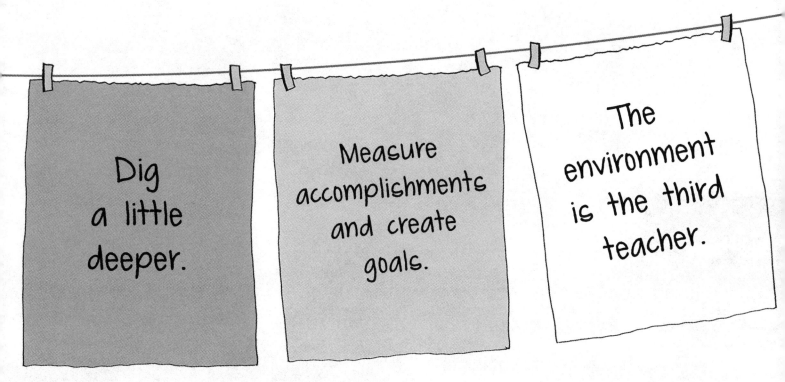

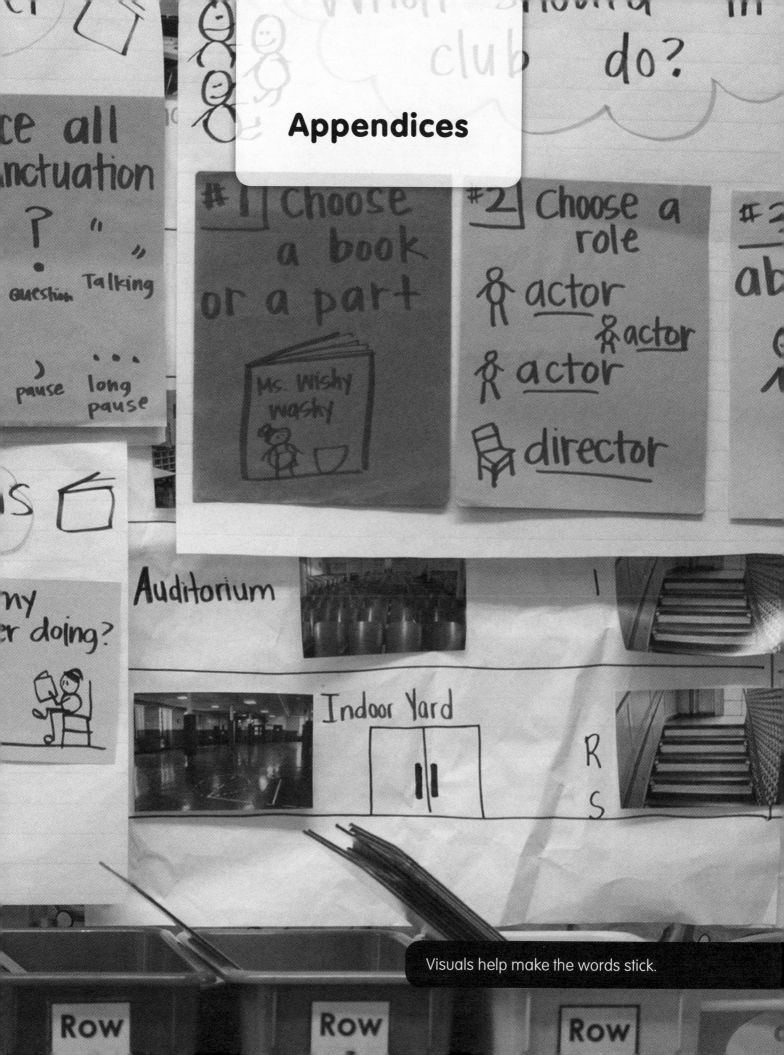

Appendices

Visuals help make the words stick.

A Field Guide to Literacy Charts

Type of Chart	Purpose	Notes	Example
Routine	Teaches a routine or behavior to students	• Often numbered • Written like a how-to • Includes photographs of students in action • Most often made at the beginning of the year	**Fig. A.** "How to Set Up for Writers' Workshop" chart
Strategy	Records a list of strategies for a big skill	• Not numbered • Students self-select the strategy that matches what they need to do • Grows over multiple lessons	**Fig. B.** A strategy chart
Process	Breaks a big skill into a sequence of steps	• Can be numbered or sometimes represented in a circle • Students need to do each of the steps to complete the process • Usually taught in one lesson	**Fig. C.** "Writers Plan Our Stories" chart
Exemplar	Shows specific strategies or skills in context	• Usually a shared or interactive writing piece • Teacher annotates where a certain skill is with a big sticky note or note in the margin	**Fig. D.** Joshua's piece of writing has been annotated by the teacher in order to use it as an exemplar.
Genre	Teaches students the elements of a specific genre	• Usually built collaboratively with students after studying some sample of the genre • Grows over multiple lessons	**Fig. E.** "Fiction Stories Have" chart

© 2012 by Marjorie Martinelli and Kristine Mraz from *Smarter Charts*. Heinemann: Portsmouth, NH.

Charts can be categorized in several ways.

Appendix A

What Should I Write on My Chart?

Tips for creating any type of chart

Step 1. Think: Does the strategy I am teaching fit on a chart I already have or a new chart? If it's a new chart, make a heading that names the big idea.

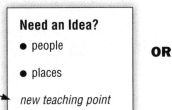

Need an Idea?
- people
- places

new teaching point

OR

New Chart?

Step 2. Reread: What are the key words or phrases in this teaching point? Underline them.

Tip: It is usually the verbs!

Writers <u>make a movie</u> for their reader when we <u>use small actions</u> in our writing.

We <u>envision</u> the moment in our mind and <u>slow down</u> our bodies and <u>write</u> what we did <u>bit by bit</u>.

Step 3. Ask myself: Is this language familiar to my students or do I need to choose different vocabulary that my children will understand?

Make a movie

Use small actions = use *itsy-bitsy* instead.

Envision = use *picture* instead.

Slow down.

Bit-by-bit = use *step-by-step* instead.

Step 4. Decide: Based on my students' reading levels, will I write a phrase or a sentence?

Make a movie with itsy-bitsy actions:

1. Picture it.

2. S-L-O-W it down.

3. Write it step-by-step.

Step 5. Choose: What visual support will I use?

Make a movie with itsy-bitsy actions:

1. Picture it.

2. S-L-O-W it down.

3. Write it step-by-step.

Areas of Teaching and Sample Goals

© 2012 by Marjorie Martinelli and Kristine Mraz from *Smarter Charts*. Heinemann: Portsmouth, NH.

Area of Teaching	And That Means . . .	Sample Goals Might Sound Like . . .
Genre	This involves teaching the elements of a specific genre to your students—for example, studying the characteristics of information books to aid students in writing their own information books.	**Writing** Students will be able to identify and use the distinguishing features of nonfiction texts in their own information books. **Reading** Students will identify and use the distinguishing features of nonfiction to read and understand grade-level nonfiction texts.
Reading and writing process	There are many different writing processes in the world, but a common one follows these steps: generate, plan, draft, revise, and edit. The reading process is often described as predict, revise, and confirm. This is true on a word level, page level, and book level.	**Writing** Students will revise writing pieces as they go so that the piece better matches the story they want to tell. **Reading** Readers will monitor as they read to make sure what they read makes sense, sounds right, and looks right.
Qualities of good reading and writing	Regardless of genre, there are qualities that make for good writing. A few of them are: focus, elaboration, craft, and voice. In reading, this might mean: fluency, deep comprehension, literal comprehension.	**Writing** Students will use varied elaboration strategies to develop tension in their stories. **Reading** Students will stop and think about the characters so that they gain a deeper understanding of the text.
Behaviors of readers and writers	Stamina, talking with partners, and building volume are all behaviors of writers and readers. This also covers teaching around problem solving.	**Writing** Students will write for thirty-five minutes every day. **Reading** Students will read for thirty-five minutes every day.

This chart shows areas of teaching and sample goals.

Appendix C

Appendix D

Self-Assessment Sheet

Teacher Asks	Child Responds	Observations
What is a chart? What is a tool? Why do we have charts and tools?		
What do you use to help you read and write?		
Can you show me a place in your reading/writing where you used a chart or tool?		
Give me a tour of the classroom. Where are some places that you go when you get stuck?		
Teach me how to use this. (Hold up a chart or tool.)		
What's hard for you? Is there anything that you could use to help you?		
What is your favorite chart? Why?		
What is a chart you do not use? Why?		
Is there any chart you wish you had to help you?		
If you could make a chart, what would you make?		

Interview questions to assess how charts are being used.

Chart Behaviors Observation Sheet

Names	Looks at Chart	Walks to Chart	Uses Individual Charts	Notes
1.				
2.				
3.				
4.				
5.				
6.				
7.				
8.				
9.				
10.				
11.				
12.				
13.				
14.				
15.				
16.				
17.				
18.				
19.				
20.				

Appendix E

Keeping track of behaviors helps teachers know how charts are being used.

Commonly Used Chart Visuals

Suggested Resources and Supply List

Resources

Chartchums.wordpress.com

Supply List

- Chart markers like Mr. Sketch, Crayola, or Sharpie Flip Chart Markers
- 6 × 8-inch sticky notes in all four fluorescent colors: neon pink, neon yellow, neon orange, and neon green (Other shapes and sizes can also be fun to have on hand when making charts memorable.)
- Fluorescent copy paper
- Repositionable or restickable glue sticks so you can turn any piece of paper into a sticky note
- A spiral sketch book (Especially for the itinerate teacher, this is an excellent container for your charts. You may want two, one for reading and one for writing. We use the 11 × 14-inch size as it fits perfectly in most backpacks and totes.)
- Chart tablets (half size, full size, blank and/or lined)

Appendix G

Bibliography

Allington, Richard. 2006. *What Really Matters for Struggling Readers*. Boston: Pearson Education.

Bruner, Jerome. 1971. *The Relevance of Education*. New York: W. W. Norton & Company.

Calkins, Lucy. 1994. *The Art of Teaching Writing*. Portsmouth, NH: Heinemann.

Cappellini, Mary. 2005. *Balancing Reading & Language Learning*. Portland, ME: Stenhouse.

Clay, Marie M. 1985. *Early Detection of Reading Difficulties: A Diagnostic Survey with Recovery Procedures*. 3d ed. Auckland, New Zealand: Heinemann.

———. 1991. *Becoming Literate: The Construction of Inner Control*. Portsmouth, NH: Heinemann.

Crews, Donald. 1991. *Bigmama's*. New York: Greenwillow.

Gandini, Lella. 1998. "Educational and Caring Spaces." In *The Hundred Languages of Children: The Reggio Emilia Approach—Advanced Reflections*, edited by Carolyn Edwards, Lella Gandini, and George Forman. Westport, CT/London: Ablex.

Gardner, Howard. 1999. *Intelligence Reframed*. New York: Basic Books.

Holdaway, Don. 1979. *The Foundations of Literacy*. Sydney: Ashton Scholastic.

Johnston, Peter. 2004. *Choice Words*. Portland, ME: Stenhouse.

Lidwell, William, Jill Butler, and Kritina Holden. 2010. *Universal Principles of Design*. Beverly, MA: Rockport Publishers.

Malaguzzi, Loris. 1998. "History, Ideas, and Basic Philosophy: An Interview with Lella Gandini." In *The Hundred Languages of Children: The Reggio Emilia Approach—Advanced Reflections*, edited by Carolyn Edwards, Lella Gandini, and George Forman. Westport, CT/London: Ablex.

Medina, John. 2008. *Brain Rules*. Seattle, WA: Pear Press.

Mermelstein, Leah. 2006. *Reading/Writing Connections in the K–2 Classroom*. Boston: Pearson Education.

Mooney, Margaret. 1995. *Developing Life-long Readers*. Wellington, New Zealand: Learning Media.

Moustafa, Margaret. 1997. *Beyond Traditional Phonics*. Portsmouth, NH: Heinemann.

Parkes, Brenda. 2000. *Read It Again*. Portland, ME: Stenhouse.

Peterson, Ralph. 1992. *Life in a Crowded Place: Making a Learning Community*. Portsmouth, NH: Heinemann.

Rasinski, Timothy. 2010. *The Fluent Reader*. 2d ed. New York: Scholastic.

Ray, Katie Wood, and Matt Glover. 2008. *Already Ready*. Portsmouth, NH: Heinemann.

Schwartz, Shanna. 2008. *Making Your Teaching Stick*. Portsmouth, NH: Heinemann.

Smith, Frank. 1983. *Joining the Literacy Club*. Portsmouth, NH: Heinemann.

Tufte, Edward R. 1990. *Envisioning Information*. Cheshire, CT: Graphics Press.

———. 2006. Beautiful Evidence. Cheshire, CT: Graphics Press.

Wolfe, Patricia. 2001. *Brain Matters*. Alexandria, VA: ASCD.

Zion, Gene. 1956, 1984. *Harry the Dirty Dog*. New York: Harper Collins.

Notes/Sketches

Notes/Sketches

Notes/Sketches

Notes/Sketches